Advances in Analytics for Learning and Teaching

Series Editors
Dirk Ifenthaler, Learning, Design and Technology
University of Mannheim
Mannheim, Baden-Württemberg, Germany

David Gibson, Teaching and Learning
Curtin University
Bentley, WA, Australia

This book series highlights the latest developments of analytics for learning and teaching as well as providing an arena for the further development of this rapidly developing field.

It provides insight into the emerging paradigms, frameworks, methods, and processes of managing change to better facilitate organizational transformation toward implementation of educational data mining and learning analytics. The series accepts monographs and edited volumes focusing on the above-mentioned scope, and covers a number of subjects. Titles in the series *Advances in Analytics for Learning and Teaching* look at education from K-12 through higher education, as well as vocational, business, and health education. The series also is interested in teaching, learning, and instructional design and organization as well as data analytics and technology adoption.

More information about this series at https://link.springer.com/bookseries/16338

Demetrios Sampson
Zacharoula Papamitsiou • Dirk Ifenthaler
Michail Giannakos • Sofia Mougiakou
Dimitra Vinatsella

Educational Data Literacy

 Springer

Demetrios Sampson
Department of Digital Systems
University of Piraeus
Piraeus, Greece

Dirk Ifenthaler
Learning, Design and Technology
University of Mannheim
Mannheim, Baden-Württemberg, Germany

Sofia Mougiakou
Department of Digital Systems
University of Piraeus
Piraeus, Greece

Zacharoula Papamitsiou
Department of Technology Management
SINTEF Digital
Trondheim, Norway

Michail Giannakos
Dept of Computer Science
Norwegian University of Science &
Technology
Trondheim, Norway

Dimitra Vinatsella
Department of Digital Systems
University of Piraeus
Piraeus, Greece

ISSN 2662-2122　　　　　　ISSN 2662-2130　(electronic)
Advances in Analytics for Learning and Teaching
ISBN 978-3-031-11707-7　　　ISBN 978-3-031-11705-3　(eBook)
https://doi.org/10.1007/978-3-031-11705-3

This Springer imprint is published by the registered company Springer Nature Switzerland AG
The registered company address is: Gewerbestrasse 11, 6330 Cham, Switzerland

Contents

List of Figures

List of Tables

About the Authors

Demetrios Sampson is Professor of Digital Systems for Teaching and Learning in the Department of Digital Systems, University of Piraeus, Greece, since 2003. He has been Professor of Learning Technologies and director of research in the School of Education, Curtin University, Australia (2015–2017), and senior researcher (1999–2003) at the Information Technologies Institute at the Centre for Research and Technology—Hellas (CERTH). He is the co-author of 350 articles in scientific books, journals, and conferences, and editor of more than 90 books, special issues in academic journals, and international conference proceedings books. He has received 10 times Best Paper Award in International Conferences on Learning Technologies. He has been a keynote/invited speaker/lecturer in more than 100 international/national conferences and/or postgraduate programs around the world. Demetrios has also been project director, principal investigator, and/or research consultant in 70 research and innovation projects with external funding at the range of 16 million€. He has supervised more than 180 honors and postgraduate students to successful completion since 2003. He has developed and delivered the first Massive Online Open Course (MOOC) on the use of educational data analytics by school teachers (Analytics for the Classroom Teacher), offered by the edX platform (a Harvard and MIT led global initiative), which has attracted more than 25,000 participants from 180 countries around the world since October 2016. He led an international university-industry consortium (Learn2Analyse) that promotes professional development in educational data literacy for online education and training professionals and higher education students, co-funded by the European Commission (Erasmus+ Knowledge Alliance Program, 2018–2021). He is the recipient of the IEEE Computer Society Distinguished Service Award (July 2012) and was named a Golden Core Member of IEEE Computer Society in recognition of his contribution to the field of learning technologies. He is also the recipient of the Golden Nikola Tesla Chain Award of the International Society for Engineering Pedagogy (IGIP) for "International outstanding achievements in the field of Engineering Pedagogy" (September 2018).

Zacharoula Papamitsiou (she/her) is a research scientist in the Department of Technology Management, SINTEF Digital. Dr. Papamitsiou holds a PhD degree from the University of Macedonia, Thessaloniki, Greece, in adapting and personalizing assessment using learning analytics. Her research interest is on learning analytics, user modeling, autonomous learning, digital transformation, human-computer interaction, and trustworthy AI. She has published more than 40 peer-reviewed papers in highly ranked journals, conferences papers, and book chapters (including *British Journal of Educational Technologies, Computers in Human Behavior, IEEE TLT, Information Systems Frontiers, LAK, UMAP*, and *ICE*); she is a reviewer in more than 10 highly ranked journals (including *Computers and Education, Computers in Human Behavior, IEEE Transactions in Learning Technologies, Journal of Computer Assisted Learning*, and *Journal of Learning Analytics*); and she has served/serves as guest editor in prestigious journals (e.g., *Frontier in Artificial Intelligence*) and in various organization committees (e.g., associate chair) and program committees. Dr. Papamitsiou is professional member of ACM and IEEE Technical Committee on Learning Technology, and founding member of the Trondheim-ACM-W Chapter. She has been involved in several projects, funded by the Norwegian Research Council, European Commission (e.g., Horizon 2020 and Erasmus+), and other national or international associations (e.g., Norwegian Ministry of Foreign Affairs, Innovation Norway, and NordForsk). In 2017, she received the Martin Wolpers Award for the research project of the most promising young researcher. Dr. Papamitsiou is also recipient of the ERCIM fellowship and has completed her postdoctoral research in the Computer Science Department at the Norwegian University of Science and Technology (NTNU).

Dirk Ifenthaler is Professor and Chair of Learning, Design, and Technology at the University of Mannheim, Germany, and UNESCO deputy chair of data science in higher education learning and teaching at Curtin University, Australia. His previous roles include professor and director of the Centre for Research in Digital Learning at Deakin University, Australia; manager of applied research and learning analytics at Open Universities, Australia; and Professor for Applied Teaching and Learning Research at the University of Potsdam, Germany. He was a 2012 Fulbright Scholar-in-Residence in the Jeannine Rainbolt College of Education at the University of Oklahoma, USA. Dirk's research focuses on the intersection of cognitive psychology, educational technology, data analytics, and organizational learning. His research outcomes include numerous co-authored books, book series, book chapters, journal articles, and international conference papers, as well as successful grant funding in Australia, Germany, and USA. He is the editor-in-chief of the Springer journal *Technology, Knowledge and Learning*. He received the 2016 Outstanding International Research Collaboration Award from AERA (American Educational Research Association), the 2015 Presidential Award from AECT (Association for Educational Communications and Technology), and the 2012 Outstanding Journal Article Award from AECT, as well as the 2006 Outstanding Dissertation Award by the University of Freiburg, Germany. He has published more than 250 journal articles, book chapters, and books and has received over 7876 citations resulting in an h-index of 45 (Google Scholar, June 2022).

Michail Giannakos is Professor of Interaction Design and Learning Technologies in the Department of Computer Science at the Norwegian University of Science and Technology (NTNU). He is the head of the Learner-Computer Interaction Laboratory, and his research focuses on the design and study of emerging technologies in online and hybrid education settings, and on developing new ways for humans to interact with interactive learning systems. Giannakos has co-authored more than 200 manuscripts published in prestigious peer-reviewed journals and conferences (including *Computers & Education*, *Computers in Human Behavior*, *IEEE Pervasive Computing*, *IEEE TLT*, *BIT*, *BJET*, *ACM IDC*, *ICLS/CSCL*, and *Interact*). Giannakos is the editor-in-chief of the *International Journal of Child-Computer Interaction* (Elsevier). He is also member of the editorial boards of *IEEE Transactions in Learning Technology*, *IEEE Transactions on Education*, *Behaviour & Information Technology*, and the *International Journal of Information Management*, and has served as a guest editor for highly recognized journals. He has served as an evaluator for the European Commission (EC) and the US-NSF, and he recently co-edited the *Multimodal Learning Analytics Handbook* (Springer) and authored a book on experimental studies in learning technology and child–computer interaction (Springer). Giannakos has worked at several research projects funded by diverse sources like the European Commission, Microsoft Research, The Research Council of Norway (RCN), US-NSF, the German agency for international academic cooperation, and Cheng Endowment. Giannakos is one of the experts in the Norwegian task force (formed by the ministry of education and research) for introducing learning analytics to Norwegian K-12 schools and universities. He is also a recipient of a Marie Curie/ERCIM fellowship and the Norwegian Young Research Talent award, and he is one of the outstanding academic fellows of NTNU (2017–2022).

Sofia Mougiakou is a computer science teacher in secondary education since 1996. She holds a BSc in informatics and telecommunications (November 1994) from the Department of Informatics and Telecommunications, National and Kapodistrian University of Athens, Greece; an MSc in electronic automation (June 1998) from the Department of Informatics and Telecommunications, National and Kapodistrian University of Athens, Greece; as well as a MSc with distinction in e-learning from the Department of Digital Systems, University of Piraeus, Greece (June 2020). She has 2 years of administrative experience as a high school principal and 10 years as head of the Center of Informatics and New Technologies of the Directorate of Secondary Education of Piraeus. She has 15 years of teaching experience as a computer science teacher in secondary education. Sofia participated as a member of the Education Committee in two co-funded European projects for teachers' professional development, as well as in the Learn2Analyze project (Erasmus+ Knowledge Alliance Program). She has several conference publications regarding the exploitation of blended learning using the Moodle Learning Platform at the high-school level. Currently, she is a PhD candidate in the Department of Digital Systems, University of Piraeus, Greece.

Dimitra Vinatsella holds a BSc in informatics and telecommunications (2003) and an MSc in communication systems and networks (2007) from National and Kapodistrian University of Athens. She began working as a product development manager at Vodafone Greece responsible to act as an overall project manager for the planning, development, roll out, and post-launch monitoring of retail commercial value added services and products. In 2007, she joined the Greek Ministry of Education, Research and Religious Affairs, as a computer science teacher, and since 2012, she has been working in a cross-functional team in the Center for Informatics and New Technologies at the Directorate of Secondary Education of Piraeus. She has a long experience in e-learning utilizing innovative technologies and learning management systems, and she has participated successfully in several scientific research European programs, including the Learn2Analyze project. Currently, she is a PhD candidate in the Department of Digital Systems, University of Piraeus, Greece.

Abbreviations

CF	Competence Framework
CP	Competence Profile
Covid-19	Coronavirus Disease 2019
CMS	Course Management Systems
DDDM	Data-Driven Decision Making
DL	Data Literacy
DPO	Data Protection Officer
CF-DS	Data Science Competence Framework
EDA	Educational Data Analytics
EDL	Educational Data Literacy
EDL CP	Educational Data Literacy Competence Profile
ESN	Erasmus Student Network
EQF	European Qualifications Framework
eTUT	e-Tutors
GDPR	General Data Protection Regulation
HEI	Higher Education Institutions
ID	Instructional Designers
LMS	Learning Management Systems
L2A	Learn2Analyze
L2A-EDL-CP	Learn2Analyze Educational Data Literacy Competence Profile
VET	Vocational Education and Training

Chapter 1
Introduction

Abstract This chapter discusses the "upskilling imperative" of educational data literacy (EDL) as fundamental to the digital readiness of educational organisations and professionals, and therefore as the rationale behind the need for extending existing professional competence frameworks for educators with new competences to accommodate the emerging field of educational data analytics. Educational data literacy is recognised as a core competence for all education professionals, including school leaders and teachers, instructional designers, and tutors of online and blended learning courses, so as to stay attuned to the new technological advances and the fast-changing labour market demands and to deal effectively with the modern social and economic challenges. Nevertheless, existing professional competence frameworks for educators pay little attention to EDL, thus missing the potential of using emerging EDL methods and tools in online and blended teaching and learning.

Keywords Educational data literacy · Educational data analytics · Teaching and learning analytics · Online and blended learning · Competence profiles · Teacher education and professional development

Digital education is recognised as a key transformative innovation for K-12 school and university teaching and learning, as well as for professional development and vocational training (OECD, 2016). As a result, *blended and online courses* are nowadays widely deployed to meet the needs of K-12, higher education, and vocational training students, as well as the needs for professional development of in-service professionals. Such courses are typically supported by *course* or *learning management systems* (CMS or LMS), which are web-based systems that organise and handle teaching and learning activities and digital educational content. The iterative process of designing, delivering, evaluating and refining high-quality online or blended courses and learning experiences is at the core *of online education and training*.

In this context, important professional roles in digital education and training, such as the *instructional designers*, who design and develop online and blended courses, and *trainers* or *tutors*, who support the delivery of these online and blended courses, require *new professional competences* compared to those assumed in traditional face-to-face education and training programs (Mandinach et al., 2015).

This is particularly relevant today as the *Covid-19 pandemic* unfolded around the world, *calling for education systems to take immediate action*. This crisis revealed significant shortcomings and inequities in access to technology and skills to effectively use technology and, in parallel, the *enormous potential of technology-supported innovation in education* (Reimers et al., 2020). Entering this new post Covid-19 era, *school organisations*, *leaders* and *teachers* are challenged with *reinventing their teaching* and *learning environments* to offer higher-quality, more accessible and inclusive teaching, learning and assessment (European Commission, 2020c) beyond the periods of emergency education (such as public health crises or natural disasters). Experiences during the period of lockdowns showed that fast and efficient responses to emergency situations depend largely on the *level of pre-existing digital capacity* (European Commission, 2020b). School teachers' preparedness to adapt to new pedagogical strategies and to get the best results in online and blended teaching and learning is fundamental. The 2020 Commission's Communication on Achieving the European Education Area by 2025 emphasises the *crucial role of teachers and trainers as cornerstones of Europe's economic and social prosperity*, since "without teachers and trainers, no innovation, no inclusion and no transformational education experiences for learners can take place" (European Commission, 2020c). It also recognises *the need for highly competent and motivated educators* who have opportunities for continuous professional development throughout their careers, also addressing teacher shortages that most EU countries face.

A recent advancement in online and blended teaching and learning is *educational data analytics (EDA)*, that is, the use of educational data generated during teaching and learning (including assessment) to better support individual learners' in online and blended courses. As a result, most CMSs and LMSs are now incorporating educational data analytics tools. However, these tools are not widely used because of the low *educational data literacy (EDL)* competences of the professionals that could be using them (i.e. instructional designers and trainers, or even K-12 school teachers adopting the flipped classroom model in their teaching).

Educational data literacy is a core competence for all *education professionals*, including school teachers, instructional designers and tutors of online and blended learning courses, as well as educational institutions' leaders. Nevertheless, existing *professional competence frameworks for educators* pay little attention to EDL, missing out the potential of using emerging EDL methods and tools in online and blended teaching and learning—*thus there is a need for extending existing professional competence frameworks for educators with new competences to accommodate the emerging field of Educational Data Literacy.*

The *Learn2Analyze* (L2A) was an Academia-Industry Knowledge Alliance that brought together four universities and three e-learning industries to tackle this challenge and explore the relevant opportunities. The content of this book has been developed within the initiative "*Learn2Analyze—An Academia-Industry Knowledge*

Alliance for enhancing Online Training Professionals' (Instructional Designers and e-Trainers) Competences in Educational Data Analytics", which was co-funded by the European Commission through the Erasmus+ Program of the European Union (Cooperation for innovation and the exchange of good practices—Knowledge Alliances, Agreement n. 2017-2733/001-001, Project No 588067-EPP-1-2017-1--EL-EPPKA2-KA).[1] More information about the project is available at www.learn2analyze.eu.

One of the main objectives of the Learn2Analyze project was to enhance existing professional competence frameworks for various digital education professionals (including, instructional designers and e-trainers of online courses), as well as educators, at large, with new educational data literacy competence descriptions for using emerging educational data analytics methods and tools. To this end, the Learn2Analyze project produced and validated a comprehensive proposal for an *Educational Data Literacy Competence Profile* (L2A-EDL-CP), where the alliance of academia and industry partners combined the pragmatic industry professional competence needs with the more rigid academic curriculum knowledge for the definition of the L2A-EDL-CP, and mobilised experts from both academia and industry for the validation of the proposed L2A-EDL-CP.

To this end, the approach undertaken involved environmental scan and analysis of (i) educational data literacy conceptual definitions and their dimensions to propose a working definition for EDL for digital education professionals, (ii) existing EDL or EDL-relevant competence frameworks to identify key EDL-competence dimensions and core competence statements per dimension, and (iii) EDL-relevant higher education and professional development courses to identify key EDL-related learning objectives which potentially can be matched to EDL competences.

The structure of this book is as follows:

Chapter 1 discusses the "upskilling imperative" of educational data literacy as fundamental for the digital-readiness of educational organisations and professionals and therefore as the rationale behind the need for extending existing professional competence frameworks for educators with new competences to accommodate the emerging field of educational data analytics.

Chapter 2 presents and analyses (i) educational data literacy conceptual definitions and their dimensions, (ii) existing EDL or EDL-relevant competence frameworks to identify key EDL-competence dimensions and core competence statements per dimension, and (iii) EDL-relevant higher education and professional development courses to identify key EDL-related learning objectives which potentially can be matched to EDL competences.

Chapter 3 presents a working definition of EDL for digital education professionals, as well as the synthesis of the Learn2Analyse Educational Data Literacy Competence Profile, which was initially developed based on the analysis of

---

[1] The European Commission's support for the production of this publication does not constitute an endorsement of the contents, which reflects the views only of the authors, and the Commission will not be held responsible for any use which may be made of the information contained therein.

Chap. 2, and it was validated through an expert-based questionnaire-driven online survey with 210 experts from higher education institutes and e-learning industry enterprises (Papamitsiou et al., 2021). The proposed revised validated competence framework consists of 6 competence dimensions and 17 competence statements which aim to describe these dimensions targeting the educational data literacy needs of digital education professionals.

Chapter 4 presents the exemplary learning outcomes for the two-dimensional L2A-EDL-CP framework and the use-case examples for indicative target groups of the L2A-EDL-CP, namely, instructional designers, e-trainers and K-12 teachers.

Finally, Chap. 5 discusses conclusions and suggestions for future plans based on the lessons learnt through the development and validation of the Learn2Analyze Educational Data Literacy Competence Profile (L2A-EDL-CP).

Chapter 2
Educational Data Literacy and Educational Data Literacy Competence Frameworks: An Environmental Scan

Abstract This chapter presents and analyzes (i) educational data literacy (EDL) conceptual definitions and their dimensions, (ii) existing EDL or EDL-relevant competence frameworks to identify key EDL competence dimensions and core competence statements per dimension, and (iii) EDL-relevant higher education and professional development courses to identify key EDL-related learning objectives which potentially can be matched to EDL competences. The definition of an Educational Data Literacy Competence Profile (EDL-CP) for key roles in digital education, including instructional designers and tutors of online and blended courses, as well as K12 school educators and leaders, at large, is recognized as an essential extension of existing relevant professional competence frameworks.

Keywords Educational data literacy · Educational data analytics · Teaching and learning analytics · Online and blended learning · Competence profiles · Teacher education and professional development

2.1 Scope

The scope of this chapter is to present and analyze (i) educational data literacy conceptual definitions and their dimensions, (ii) existing EDL or EDL-relevant competence frameworks to identify key EDL competence dimensions and core competence statements per dimension, and (iii) EDL-relevant higher education and professional development courses to identify key EDL-related learning objectives which potentially can be matched to EDL competences.

The proliferation of data in our daily lives and the use of data to empower our decision-making (Mortier et al., 2021) have positioned data literacy as an important life competence. ***Competence*** is defined as ***a set of skills, knowledge, and attitudes*** that are possessed or need to be acquired to perform an activity within a specific context, whereas performance may range from the basic level of proficiency to the highest levels of excellence (Sampson & Fytros, 2008). In the context of professional development, competence is the capacity to apply a set of related skills,

D. Sampson et al., *Educational Data Literacy*, Advances in Analytics for Learning and Teaching, https://doi.org/10.1007/978-3-031-11705-3_2

knowledge, and attitudes for the successful performance of "critical job functions" in a given job setting (UNIDO, 2015). As such, a ***Competence Profile (CP)*** captures and describes the ***set of competences needed for a particular job or role*** in a certain profession. Thus, it can be used for the design of professional development courses as well as for the building of competence assessment and course accreditation instruments in professional learning.

The definition of an Educational Data Literacy Competence Profile ***for key roles in Digital Education***, including instructional designers and tutors of online and blended courses, as well as K12 school educators and leaders, at large, is recognized as an essential extension of existing relevant professional competence frameworks (Redecker, 2017; European Commission, 2016, 2018, 2020b; UNESCO, 2018).

2.2 Educational Data Literacy Conceptual Definitions

This section presents an environmental scan on the conceptual definition of educational data literacy. The environmental scan was conducted after an extensive and iterative search of the international databases of academic resources and publishers. Key concepts related to EDL (i.e., *educational data literacy, educational data literacy framework, educational data literacy competences, data literacy, data literacy framework, educational data analytics use, use of educational data for teaching, use of educational data for instruction, use of educational data for instructional design, educational data-driven decision-making, educational data-driven instructional design, educational data-driven courses, educational data usage for training*) were scanned in (a) academic publication databases (i.e., Web of Science; ERIC; Scopus; Google Scholar; Sciencedirect), (b) selected academic journals and conference proceedings (e.g., IEEE International Conference on Advanced Learning Technologies, Learning Analytics, and Knowledge Conference), and (c) simple Google search.[1] We also searched for grey literature and identified articles and white papers. As this is an emerging field, we generally found that the courses and workshops and associations and organizations were more current. The time frame of the search was bound within the period between 2005 and 2018, in which the emergence of data literacy has grown.

As the scope of the environmental scan was to develop a *common understanding* and a *working definition of educational data literacy*, as well as to build a grounded proposal for an EDL competence profile for digital teaching and learning professionals and K12 school educators and leaders, at the end of the resource collection stage, we determined the criteria for inclusion/exclusion of the gathered resources. The identification of cases to be included in this collection depended highly on the relevance of the scope of this study. Although comprehensive examples of EDL

---

[1] The simple Google search facilitated the identification of published research work—beyond the academic articles—as well as the identification of the professional development courses.

initiatives have been collected, a second step in the selection of the works to include in the review was aimed at reducing the body of cases under what constituted a "framework," i.e., any organized conceptualization of the competences and sub-competences related to EDL. As such, emphasis was given to works reporting on existing EDL or EDL-relevant competence frameworks, especially the ones that provide detailed competence statements, as they are the core references to analyze.

2.2.1 Educational Data and Data-Driven Decision-Making in Educational Settings

Educational data can be broadly defined as *"information that is collected and organized to represent **some aspect of schools**. This could include [...] any relevant information about students, parents, schools, and teachers derived from qualitative and quantitative methods of analysis"* (Lai & Schildkamp, 2013, p. 10). Beyond the common misconception that educational data is restricted to students' grades on national and standardized exams, the above definition suggests that educational data comprises *a wide range of data* generated by *various and multiple sources*, both internal (school-wide and classroom-specific data) and external (state and/or district data) to the school.

Ikemoto and Marsh (2007) categorized educational data into *input data* (e.g., school expenditures, student demographics), *process data* (e.g., data on financial operations, data on the quality of instruction), *outcome data* (e.g., dropout rates, student test scores), and *satisfaction data* (e.g., opinions from teachers, students, parents, or the community). Extending this categorization of educational data, Lai and Schildkamp (2013) proposed a broader layout that includes *context data* (e.g., curriculum, school human resources, infrastructure, financial plans, school culture), *input data* (e.g., student characteristics like demographics and prior academic performance, and teacher characteristics like teacher competences, academic qualifications, or professional experience), *process data* (e.g., lesson plans, methods of assessments, classroom management), and *outcome data* (e.g., students' achievements, wellbeing, social and emotional development).

Having as an objective the *improvement of students' learning and schools' performance*, the U.S. Department of Education and the Institute of Education Sciences suggested data-driven decision-making (DDDM) as a process that involves stakeholders (i.e., educators, principals, and administrators) who systematically collect and analyze various types of educational data *to inform and guide a range of decisions* and reconsiderations (through reflection) towards achieving this objective (Hamilton et al., 2009). DDDM in schools has been defined as "the systematic collection, analysis, examination, and interpretation of data to inform practice and policy in educational settings" (Mandinach, 2012, p.71). Moreover, Marsh and Farrell (2015, p. 3) defined DDDM as a process that "refers to teachers, principals, and administrators systematically collecting and analyzing various types of data

[...] to guide a range of decisions to help improve the success of students and schools." Adopting a similar perspective, Schildkamp and Kuiper (2010, p.482) argued that DDDM concerns "systematically analyzing existing data sources within the school, applying outcomes of analyses to innovate teaching, curricula, and school performance, and implementing (e.g., genuine improvement actions) and evaluating these innovations." Essentially, DDDM in schools refers to a continuous cycle of identifying, collecting, combining, analyzing, interpreting, and acting upon educational data from different sources, in order to report, evaluate, and improve the resources, processes, and outcomes of schools. This conception of DDDM implies a set of *"data literacy"* competences that may be *needed to engage in meaningful data use* and move from data, to information, to knowledge, to action (Knapp et al., 2006; Means et al., 2011).

2.2.2   *Data Literacy and Educational Data Literacy*

The overall human *capacity to understand, learn from, and use data* as part of everyday thinking and reasoning for solving real-world problems is synopsized under the term data literacy (DL). Vahey et al. (2006, p.1) proposed that DL *"includes the ability to formulate and answer questions using data as part of evidence-based thinking; use appropriate data, tools, and representations to support this thinking; interpret information from data; develop and evaluate data-based inferences and explanations; and use data to solve real problems and communicate their solutions."* Mandinach and Gummer (2013, p. 30) define DL as *"the ability to understand and use data effectively to inform decisions."* According to Prado and Marzal (2013), DL enables individuals to access, interpret, critically assess, manage (i.e., preserve and curate), handle, and ethically use data. Much like literacy as a general concept, DL focuses on the competencies involved in working with data (e.g., read, understand, create, and communicate data) through an inquiry process, with consideration of ethical use of data.

Further focusing on DL in the educational setting, i.e., educational data literacy, Means et al. (2011) identified five skill areas that cover the *different aspects of data use that teachers need to master* if they are to use student data to improve instruction, including data location, data comprehension, data interpretation, question posing, and data use for instructional decision-making.

Love (2012) proposed that EDL is *"the ability to accurately observe, analyze, and respond to a variety of different kinds of data for the purpose of continuously improving teaching and learning in the classroom and school."* In a broader definition, the North Carolina Department of Public Instruction (2013) considered one's level of understanding of how to find, evaluate, and use data to inform teaching and learning under the term of EDL, whereas a data-literate educator should possess the knowledge to gather, analyze, and graphically convey information and data to support decision- making at various levels of the educational process.

From a similar perspective, the Data Quality Campaign (2014) raised the ethical dispositions that data-literate educators should adopt when continuously and effectively accessing, interpreting, acting on, and communicating multiple types of data from state, local, classroom, and other sources to improve outcomes for students, in a manner appropriate to educators' professional roles and responsibilities. According to Mandinach and Gummer (2013, p. 30), EDL is defined as *"the ability to understand and use data effectively to inform decisions [...] composed of a specific skill set and knowledge base that enables educators to transform data into information and ultimately into actionable knowledge."* In this definition, the authors determine the *skill set* to include *"knowing how to identify, collect, organize, analyze, summarize, and prioritize data,"* and the **knowledge base** to include *"how to develop hypotheses, identify problems, interpret the data, and determine, plan, implement, and monitor courses of action."* According to this definition, EDL is grounded on (a) *a set of skills* and (b) *a base of knowledge* that facilitates *educators* in improving teaching and learning through data- driven reflection and *educational leaders* in improving educational institutions' performance through data-driven evidence analysis. More recently, Ridsdale et al. (2015, p.2) define EDL as *"the ability to collect, manage, evaluate, and apply data, in a critical manner."* Furthermore, according to Wolff et al. (2016, p. 23), EDL is *"the ability to ask and answer real-world questions from large and small data sets through an inquiry process, with consideration of ethical use of data. It is based on core practical and creative skills [...] that include the abilities to select, clean, analyze, visualize, critique, and interpret data, as well as to communicate stories from data and to use data as part of a design process"*.

Table 2.1 summarizes the key definitions of educational data literacy as presented in the literature.

2.3 Educational Data Literacy Competence Frameworks

2.3.1 Educational Data Literacy Competence Frameworks: Environmental Scan

This section presents an environmental scan on *educational data literacy competence frameworks*. Our initial environment scan identified five major educational data literacy competence frameworks. Each framework consists of different numbers of conceptual dimensions and covers the competences that correspond to each one of these dimensions accordingly. Furthermore, a set of tasks that are linked to these competences is proposed by the research groups/authors in most cases.

Ridsdale et al. (2015) proposed an EDL competence framework consisting of *five dimensions*, namely, (1) conceptual framework, (2) data collection, (3) data management, (4) data evaluation, and (5) data application. The authors defined the core skills and competences that comprise EDL, using a *thematic analysis of the elements* of data literacy described in peer-reviewed literature. The included terms

Table 2.1 Key definitions of educational data literacy

Initiative	EDL definition
Means et al. (2011)	Skills in data location, data comprehension, data interpretation, question posing, and data use for instructional decision-making.
Love (2012)	The ability to accurately observe, analyze, and respond to a variety of different kinds of data for the purpose of continuously improving teaching and learning in the classroom and school.
North Carolina Department of Public Instruction (2013)	One's level of understanding of how to find, evaluate, and use data to inform teaching and learning - a data-literate educator should possess the knowledge to gather, analyze, and graphically convey information and data to support decision-making at various levels of the educational process.
Mandinach and Gummer (2013)	The ability to understand and use data effectively to inform decisions […] composed of a specific skill set and knowledge base that enables educators to transform data into information and ultimately into actionable knowledge.
Data Quality Campaign (2014)	Data-literate educators continuously, effectively, and ethically access, interpret, act on, and communicate multiple types of data from state, local, classroom, and other sources to improve outcomes for students in a manner appropriate to educators' professional roles and responsibilities.
Ridsdale et al. (2015)	The ability to collect, manage, evaluate, and apply data, in a critical manner.
Wolff et al. (2016)	The ability to ask and answer real-world questions from large and small data sets through an inquiry process, with consideration of ethical use of data. It is based on core practical and creative skills […] that include the abilities to select, clean, analyze, visualize, critique, and interpret data, as well as to communicate stories from data and to use data as part of a design process.

are *broadly defined* and involve a variety of elements considered core to EDL. The competencies and their skills, knowledge, and expected tasks are organized under the top-level elements of the EDL definition (data, collect, manage, evaluate, apply) and are categorized as conceptual competencies, core competencies, and advanced competencies. Figure 2.1 illustrates the EDL CF proposed by Ridsdale et al. (2015). In this figure, the blue color corresponds to conceptual competencies, the green color is used to describe core competencies, and the red color is used for annotating advanced competencies.

Mandinach and Gummer (2016) provided a broader definition of what they call data literacy *for teaching*: "*the ability to transform information into actionable instructional knowledge and practices by collecting, analyzing, and interpreting all types of data (assessment, school climate, behavioral, snapshot, longitudinal, moment-to-moment, and so on) to help determine instructional steps. It combines an understanding of data with standards, disciplinary knowledge and practices, curricular knowledge, pedagogical content knowledge, and an understanding of how children learn*" (p. 367). In line with this definition, their framework for data literacy for teaching combines *seven key knowledge areas* that integrate with *five data use aspects* in the inquiry process. The knowledge areas include (a) content knowledge, (b) general pedagogical knowledge, (c) curriculum knowledge, (d)

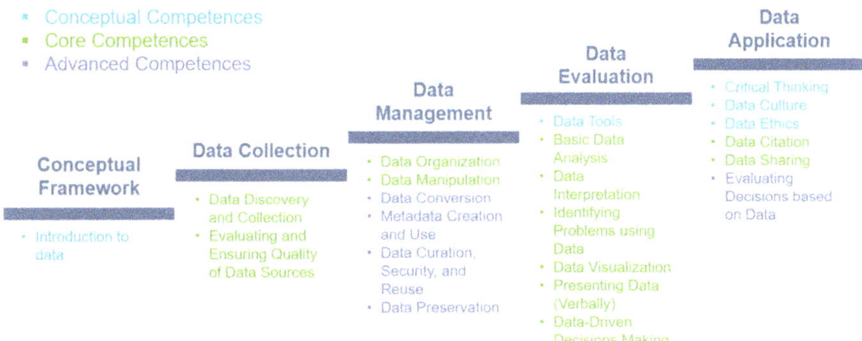

Fig. 2.1 The EDL CF dimensions as proposed by Ridsdale et al. (2015)

pedagogical content knowledge, (e) knowledge of learners and their characteristics, (f) knowledge of educational contexts, and (g) knowledge of educational ends, purposes, and values. All these knowledge dimensions *can be efficiently applicable* in DDDM only if the educators are *skillful in handling data* and given that the technological tools to support the development of DDDM are available. The data use for the teaching domain is then comprised of five components under which we have associated specific knowledge and skills. The five data use domains include the following: (1) identify problems and frame questions, (2) use data, (3) transform data into information, (4) transform information into a decision, and (5) evaluate outcomes. Figure 2.2 illustrates the EDL CF proposed by Mandinach and Gummer (2016).

Furthermore, Means et al. (2011) identified *five (5) dimension* of educational data literacy: (1) data location (i.e., finding the relevant and available pieces of data in the data system or display), (2) data comprehension (i.e., understanding what the data signify), (3) data interpretation (i.e., figuring out what the data mean), (4) data use for instructional decision-making (i.e., selecting an instructional approach to address the situation identified through the data), and (5) question posing (i.e., framing instructionally relevant questions that can be addressed by the data in the system) (Fig. 2.3). For evaluating these five dimensions, the research team collected *data scenario responses (interviews) from individual teachers and small groups* of school staff. Conducting both individual and group interviews provided information about how teachers reason independently about data as well as about how they build on each other's understanding when they explore data in small groups.

In another attempt, Marsh (2012) outlined an EDL competence model of *five (5) components of the data use process*, including (1) accessing or collecting data, (2) filtering, organizing, or analyzing data into information, (3) combining information with expertise and understanding to build knowledge, (4) knowing how to respond and taking action or adjusting one's practice, and (5) assessing the effectiveness of these actions or outcomes that result. The author introduced this framework in order to facilitate the understanding of what research tells us about *interventions designed to support the process of educational data use* and to *identify where there are*

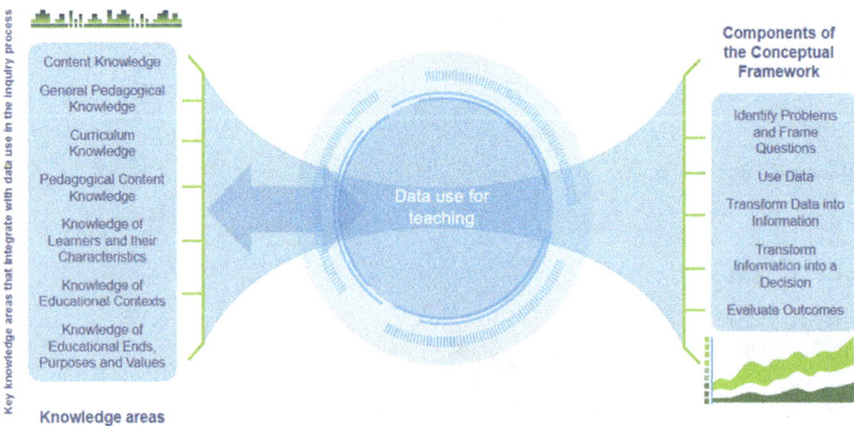

Fig. 2.2 The EDL CF dimensions as proposed by Mandinach and Gummer (2016)

Fig. 2.3 The EDL CF dimensions as proposed by Means et al. (2011)

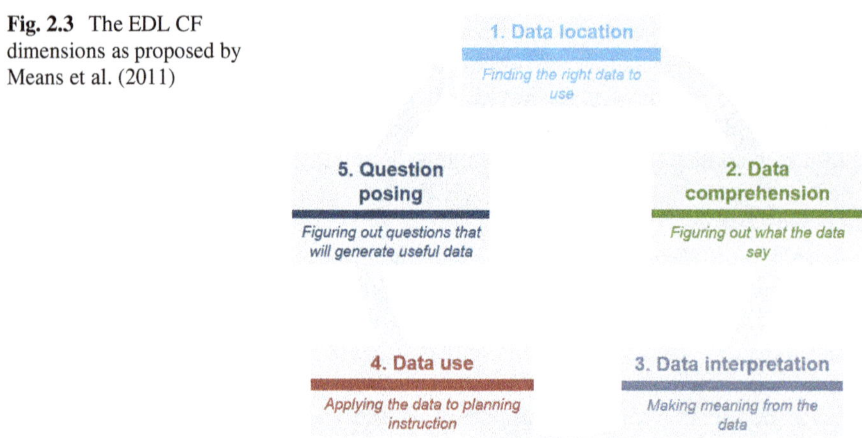

possible gaps. More specifically, the core questions the framework targets concern the dimensions or core features of these interventions, the types of data and data users that were targeted, the implementation of interventions, as well as their outcomes. Figure 2.4 presents the framework envisaged by Marsh (2012).

In addition, the EDL framework suggested by Prado and Marzal (2013) was inspired by the general structure of information literacy standards and includes *five generic dimensions*: (1) understanding data, (2) finding and/or obtaining data, (3) reading, interpreting, and evaluating data, (4) managing data, and (5) using data (Fig. 2.5). Additionally, the framework associates a number of competences with each dimension and translates these competencies into instructional topics or units to facilitate interpretation and direct implementation.

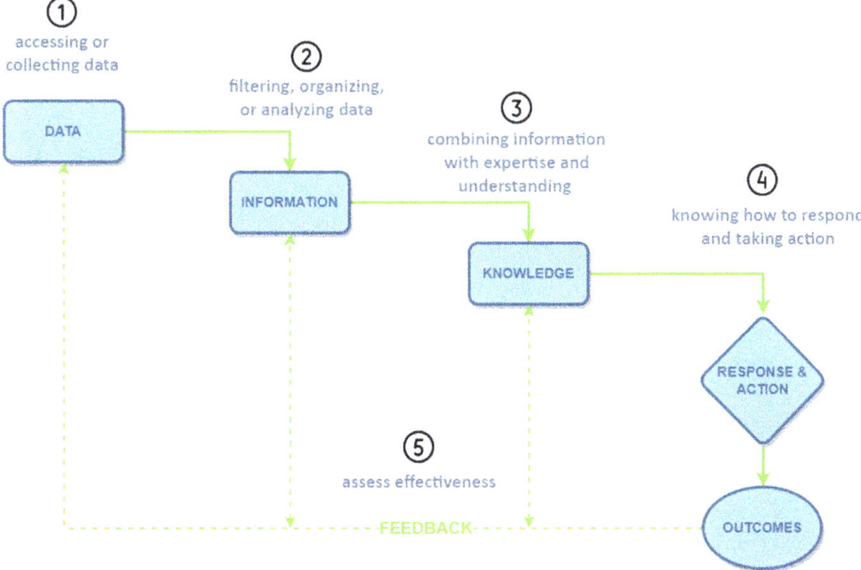

Fig. 2.4 The EDL CF dimensions as proposed by Marsh (2012)

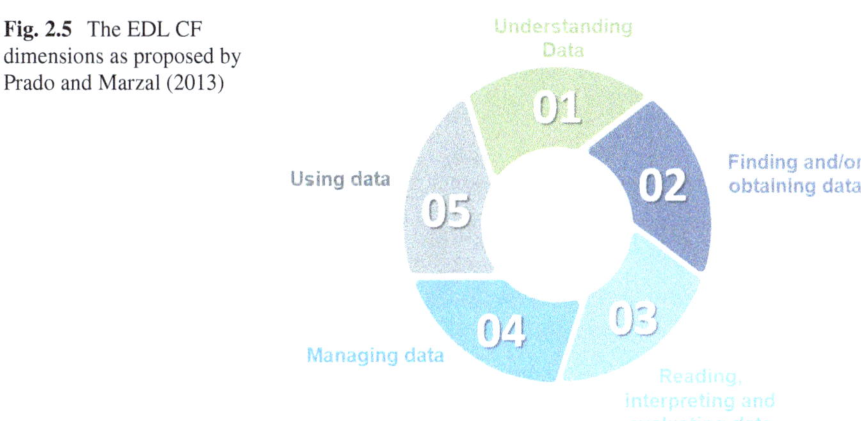

Fig. 2.5 The EDL CF dimensions as proposed by Prado and Marzal (2013)

Based on the analysis above, Table 2.2 demonstrates a synopsis and synthesis of EDL competence dimensions in relation to existing EDL competence frameworks and EDL key definitions.

Based on this table, it can be seen that most of the existing EDL competence frameworks share common data-related competence dimensions, namely:

(a) Data location, access and collection (in 7 out of 10),
(b) Data interpretation and transformation to information (in 8 out of 10),
(c) Data use, application, and action upon (in 10 out of 10),

Table 2.2 EDL competence dimensions in existing EDL competence frameworks[a]/definitions

	Identified EDL dimension	EDL key definitions							EDL CFs		
		1	2	3	4	5	6	7	8	9[b]	10
Generic	Professionalism								X		
	Content-curriculum								X		
	Pedagogy								X		
	Ethics	X			X						
	Question posing/identify problems	X						X	X		
Data -related	Data location/access/collection	X		X	X		X	X		X	X
	Data comprehension					X		X			X
	Data interpretation/transform to information	X		X	X	X		X	X	X	X
	Data use/application/act on	X	X	X	X	X	X	X	X	X	X
	Data analysis	X	X	X						X	
	Data observation		X								
	Data evaluation	X		X			X		X	X	X
	Data management	X					X			X	X

[a][1] Wolff et al. (2016); [2] Love (2012); [3] North Carolina Department of Public Instruction (2013); [4] Data Quality Campaign (2014); [5] Mandinach and Gummer (2013); [6] Ridsdale et al. (2015); [7] Means et al. (2011); [8] Mandinach and Gummer (2016); [9] Marsh (2012); [10] Prado and Marzal (2013)
[b]This framework consists of five dimensions that by themselves are competence statements and that are not further particularized into more fine-grained statements

(d) Data analysis (in 4 out of 10),
(e) Data evaluation (in 6 out of 10) and
(f) Data management (in 4 out of 10).

Furthermore, throughout the EDL process, question posing and problem identification (in 3 out of 10), as well as data ethics (in 2 out of 10), should be also considered.

2.3.2   Analysis of Educational Data Literacy Competence Frameworks in Relation to Their Capacity to Support Digital Education Professionals

In the previous section, the initial environment scan identified five major educational data literacy competence frameworks. This section presents the analysis of the EDL competence frameworks in relation to their capacity to support key roles in digital education, including instructional designers and tutors of online and blended learning courses, as well as K12 school teachers and leaders. The framework proposed by Marsh (2012) is omitted from the analysis, as it consists of five dimensions that are not further particularized into more fine-grained statements.

The objective of this section is to cover in detail the specific competence statements proposed in the four selected existing frameworks that are associated to each EDL dimension identified in the respective approaches. The analysis of these frameworks will be useful to deeper understanding of which exact competences are necessary to be possessed or acquired by digital education professionals to effectively inform their role in digital teaching and learning.

2.3.2.1   EDL-CF1: Strategies and Best Practices for Data Literacy Education (Ridsdale et al. (2015))

Ridsdale et al. (2015) synthesized a set of skills and abilities that together comprise various levels of data literacy, presented in a *data literacy competencies matrix*, organized by the *five (5) core dimensions* they proposed in their data literacy definition (data, collection, management, evaluation, application). The objective of this matrix was to constitute *a standard for assessing and evaluating levels of data literacy* and to inform the creation of learning outcomes in data literacy education. Elaborating more on the dimensions of this proposal, the *conceptual framework* dimension here has been introduced to capture the general knowledge and understanding about data and the uses and applications of data. In a sense, it corresponds to an understanding of how instructional decisions are informed by data and of how to use educational data in support of evidence-based decision-making. This dimension includes one (1) competence statement. The *data collection* dimension covers skills and knowledge related to data discovery and collection from multiple educational sources by ensuring the quality of datasets and includes two (2) competence statements. In a way, both roles should be able to recognize faulty information and create "valid, data-based arguments" (Vahey et al., 2012, p. 183). The *data management* concept pertains to the skills that mostly relate to data organization, preservation, manipulation, curation, and security and involves six (6) relevant competence statements. This dimension encompasses these skills and knowledge that allow IDs and eTUTs to have control over the data in the data-based decision-making processes. The *data evaluation* construct focuses on skills that are related to data analysis, presentation, interpretation, and making instructional decisions from data, and it contains seven (7) competence statements in total. Finally, the *data application* dimension is orientated to knowledge and skills that are needed to share and cite data, to evaluate decisions based on data, and to work with data in an ethical manner, and it includes six (6) competence statements. The research team followed a thematic analysis of the elements of data literacy described in peer-reviewed literature and concluded that there are *23 competencies* (categorized as conceptual competencies, core competencies, and advanced competencies) with *64 core skills, knowledge, and expected tasks*. In particular, the exact competence statements (with specific skills) per dimension are illustrated in Table 2.3.

Table 2.3 Data-related competence dimensions and competence statements of the EDL CF1

EDL CF1 (Ridsdale et al., 2015)	
EDL competence dimensions 5	EDL competence statements 23
Conceptual framework	Introduction to data (*knowledge and understanding of data; knowledge and understanding of the uses and applications of data*)
Data collection	Data discovery and collection (*performs data exploration; identifies useful data; collects data*)
	Evaluating and ensuring quality of data and sources (*critically assesses sources of data for trustworthiness; critically evaluates quality of datasets for errors or problems*)
Data management	Data organization (*knowledge of basic data organization methods and tools; assesses data organization requirements; organizes data*)
	Data manipulation (*assesses methods to clean data; identifies outliers and anomalies; cleans data*)
	Data conversion from format to format (*knowledge of different data types and conversion methods; converts data from one format or file type to another*)
	Metadata creation and use (*creates metadata descriptors; assigns appropriate metadata Descriptors to original data sets*)
	Data curation, security, and re-use (*assesses data curation requirements; assess data security requirements; curates data*)
	Data preservation (*assesses requirements for preservation; assesses methods and tools for data preservation; preserves data*)
Data evaluation	Data tools (*knowledge of data analysis tools and techniques; selects appropriate data analysis tool or technique; applies data analysis tools and techniques*)
	Basic data analysis (develops analysis plans; applies analysis methods and tools; conducts exploratory analysis; evaluates results of analysis; compares results of analysis with other findings)
	Data interpretation - understanding data (reads and understands charts, tables, and graphs; identifies key take-away points, and integrates this with other important information; identifies discrepancies within the data)
	Identifying problems using data (uses data to identify problems in practical situations; uses data to identify higher level problems)
	Data visualization (creates meaningful tables to organize and visually present data; creates meaningful graphical representations of data; evaluates effectiveness of graphical representations; critically assesses graphical representations for accuracy and misrepresentation of data)
	Presenting data (verbally) (*assess the desired outcome(s) for presenting the data; assesses audience needs and familiarity with subject(s); utilizes meaningful tables and visualizations to communicate data; presents arguments and/or outcomes clearly and coherently*)
	Data driven decisions making (DDDM) (*prioritizes information garnered from data; converts data into actionable information; weighs the merit and impacts of possible solutions-decisions; implements decisions-solutions*)

(continued)

Table 2.3 (continued)

EDL CF1 (Ridsdale et al., 2015)	
EDL competence dimensions 5	EDL competence statements 23
Data application	Critical thinking (*aware of high level issues and challenges associated with data; thinks critically when working with data*)
	Data culture (*recognizes the importance of data; supports an environment that fosters critical use of data for learning, research, and decision-making*)
	Data ethics (*aware of legal and ethical issues associated with data; applies and works with data in an ethical manner*)
	Data citation (*knowledge of widely-accepted data citation methods; creates correct citations for secondary data sets*)
	Data sharing (*assesses methods and platforms for sharing data; shares data legally, and ethically*)
	Evaluating decisions based on data (*collects follow-up data to assess effectiveness of decisions or solutions based upon data; conducts analysis of follow-up data; compares results of analysis with other findings; evaluates decisions or solutions based on data; retains original conclusions or decisions, or implements new decisions/solutions*)

2.3.2.2 EDL-CF2: Conceptual Framework for Data Literacy for Teachers DLFT (Mandinach & Gummer, 2016)

The conceptual framework introduced by Mandinach and Gummer (2016) includes seven (7) key knowledge areas that integrate with *five (5) data-related components* throughout the inquiry process. The five data-related dimensions of this framework have been associated with specific knowledge and skills and include the following: identify problems and frame questions, use data, transform data into information, transform information into a decision, and evaluate outcomes. Specifically, the first dimension (*identify problems/frame questions*) focuses on how educators identify the problems, topics, issues, or questions to be addressed and includes five (5) statements. The *use data* component consists of twenty-seven (27) statements and pertains to the fundamental knowledge and skills that most directly relate to actual data use. This dimension covers an extensive area of skills educators should acquire, varying from identification of data sources to developing sound assessment design and implementation and from understanding how to analyze data to articulating inferences and conclusions from the analyzed information. The research team point outs that there might be some degree of overlap in these sub-components and elements. The *transform data into information* dimension is essentially about moving data toward information on which actions can be taken using the learning context to make meaning and inform decisions and includes nine (9) competence statements. The *transform information into decision* construct covers the sets of knowledge and skills a teacher should acquire regarding the instructional steps that should be taken based on the inquiry cycle. Five (5) statements were identified for this dimension.

Finally, the *evaluate outcomes* dimension pertains to examining the impact of the decision-making process, employing a total of five (5) statements. The *competence statements* identified in this framework were *53 in total* and are mapped to each data-related dimension as shown in Table 2.4.

Table 2.4 Data-related dimensions with competence statements of the EDL CF2

EDL CF2 (Mandinach & Gummer, 2016)	
EDL dimensions 5	EDL competence statements 53
Identify problems/ frame questions	Articulate a problem of practice (*identify the problem and explain the issue or question*)
	Understand the context at the student level (*contextualize the learning, behavioral, or motivation issues*)
	Understand the context at the school level
	Involve other participants or stakeholders
	Understand student privacy (*protection of student privacy and confidentiality*)
Use data	Identify possible sources of data
	Understand the purposes of different data sources
	Understand how to generate data
	Understand assessment
	Use formative and summative assessments
	Develop sound assessment design and implementation
	Understand data properties
	Use multiple measures/sources of data
	Use qualitative and quantitative data
	Understand specificity of data to question/problem
	Understand what data are appropriate
	Understand data quality (*validity, timeliness, and consistency of the data*)
	Understand elements of data accuracy, appropriateness, and completeness
	Understand how to access data
	Find, locate, access, and retrieve data
	Use technologies to support data use (*data warehouses, assessment systems, student information systems, and other relevant technologies that provide access to, analysis, and reporting of data*)
	Understand how to analyze data
	Understand statistics and psychometrics
	Manage data
	Organize data
	Prioritize data
	Examine data (*scrutinize or inspect them in a meaningful way to address a question, hypothesis, or issue*)
	Integrate data
	Manipulate data
	Drill down into data
	Aggregate data
	Disaggregate data

(continued)

Table 2.4 (continued)

EDL CF2 (Mandinach & Gummer, 2016)	
EDL dimensions 5	EDL competence statements 53
Transform data into information	Consider the impact and consequences
	Generate hypothetical connections to instruction
	Test assumptions
	Understand how to interpret data (*give meaning to data—explanations*)
	Understand and use data displays and representations
	Assess patterns and trends
	Probe for causality
	Use statistics
	Synthesize diverse data
	Articulate inferences and conclusions
	Summarize and explain data
Transform information into a decision	Determine next instructional steps
	Monitor student performance
	Diagnose what students need
	Make instructional adjustments.
	Understand the context for the decision
Evaluate outcomes	Re-examine the original question or problem
	Compare performance pre- and post-decision
	Monitor changes in classroom practices
	Monitor student changes in performance
	Consider the need for iterative decision cycles

2.3.2.3   EDL-CF3: Teachers' Ability to Use Data to Inform Instruction (Means et al., 2011)

The framework developed by Means et al. (2011) consists of *five (5) data-related dimensions*, focusing on better understanding teachers' strengths and weaknesses in working with data and towards informing the design of more effective teacher training and professional development. Specifically, these dimensions include data location, data comprehension, data interpretation, data use for instructional decision-making, and question posing.

More precisely, *data location* refers to the educators' ability to find relevant data that will be used to inform their decisions about students and includes two (2) competence statements. *Data comprehension* is about making sense of the data and is particularized in four (4) competence statements. *Data interpretation* refers to going beyond comprehension per se to interpreting the meaning of the data and involves four (4) competence statements. *Data use for instructional decision-making* concerns the abilities that teachers have to plan and provide differentiated instruction, tailored to the needs of the students, through techniques. Three (3) statements were identified in this dimension. Finally, *question posing* refers to forming a question about a set of data and expressing it as a data query and includes three (3) related statements. The research team examined the perceptions of 50 individual teachers and 72 small groups regarding how they think about student data in schools. The research was based on the assumption that a detailed description of teachers' thinking can be proved helpful to inform those who are responsible for training teachers in data-driven decision-making about the kinds of difficulties and misconceptions teachers are likely to encounter. In the same report, the authors provide material that can be used in training teachers on the use of data to guide instruction. Table 2.5 describes the *16 competence statements* of this approach.

2.3.2.4   EDL-CF4: Incorporating Data Literacy into Information Literacy Programs (Prado & Marzal, 2013)

The framework introduced by Prado and Marzal (2013) focuses on the data literacy competences that should be covered when designing instruction. The framework was inspired by the general structure of information literacy standards and includes most of the common competences identified by the authors in their literature scan. Specifically, in the presented approach, the framework consists of *five (5) generic data-related dimensions*: understanding data; finding/obtaining data; reading, interpreting, and evaluating data; managing data, and using data. Regarding the first dimension, *understanding data* refers to general knowledge and awareness of data, how they are generated and what the different types and sources of data are, and it includes two (2) related competence statements. The second dimension, *finding/*

Table 2.5 Data-related dimensions with competence statements of the EDL CF3

EDL CF3 (Means et al., 2011)	
EDL dimensions 5	EDL competence statements 16
Data location	Finding relevant data in a complex table or graph Manipulating data from a complex table or graph to support reasoning Moving fluently between alternative representations of data understanding a histogram
Data comprehension	Understanding a histogram Interpreting a contingency table Distinguishing between cross-sectional and longitudinal data examining score distributions
Data interpretation	Understanding the effect of outliers Appreciating limits on generalizability Understanding measurement error
Data use for instructional decision-making	Understanding the value of subscale scores Providing differentiated instruction based on data Synthesizing data from different sources
Question posing	Aligning questions with purpose and data Forming queries that lead to actionable data Appreciating the value of multiple measures

obtaining data, pertains to the skills required to access and assess data sources, and it also enumerates two (2) competence statements. The third dimension, reading, interpreting, and evaluating data, concerns the necessary competences that are relevant to presenting data and to critically evaluating them. In this framework, the authors suggest two (2) statements in this dimension. Regarding the *managing data* dimension, it is related to metadata data management repositories and data reuse and is synopsized in one (1) competence statement. Finally, the *using* data dimension—with three (3) statements—covers skills and knowledge that are needed to properly and ethically handle and synthesize data. The 10 competence statements included in this framework and assigned to each dimension are illustrated in Table 2.6.

2.3.3   Analysis of Existing Data-Related Ethics Frameworks

As the ethical consideration of data throughout the data-driven decision-making process is acknowledged as a core dimension of EDL, the analysis of data-related ethics frameworks was performed, as well. Although some authors put emphasis on

Table 2.6 Data-related dimensions with competence statements of the EDL CF4

EDL CF4 (Prado & Marzal, 2013)	
EDL dimensions	EDL competence statements
5	10
Understanding data	Knowing what is meant by data and be aware of the various possible types of data
	Data in society: a tool for knowledge and innovation
Finding and/or obtaining data	Data sources (*awareness of the possible data sources, ability to evaluate them and select the ones most relevant to an informational need or a given problem*)
	Obtaining data (*detect when a given problem or need cannot be (totally or partially) solved with the existing data and obtain new one*)
Reading, interpreting, and evaluating data	Reading and interpreting data (*knowing the various forms in which data can be presented (written, numerical or graphic), and their respective conventions, and be able to interpret them*)
	Evaluating data
Managing data	Data and metadata collection and management (*aware of the need to save the data selected or generated and of descriptive or other data associated therewith, for due identification, management and subsequent reuse*)
	Data handling (*prepare data for analysis, analyze them in keeping with the results sought and know how to use the necessary tools*)
Using data	Producing elements for data synthesis (*producing elements for data synthesis*)
	Ethical use of data

data ethics, the majority fail to make note of it. However, in order for IDs and eTUTs to understand and critically think about the larger issues regarding EDL, they must have an understanding and awareness of the ethics surrounding data. This section presents the competence statements related to data ethics as a synthesis of statements from existing data-related ethics frameworks. It should be noted that none of the existing EDL CFs provides explicit competence statements regarding the data-related ethics dimension. Thus, we searched for more general data-related ethics frameworks that contain relevant statements.

Specifically, six (6) data-related ethics frameworks were identified during the scan of relevant literature. Table 2.7 summarizes the competences that concern the ethical treatment of data.

As seen from this table, all data-related ethics frameworks highlight the need to make use of informed consent when it has to do with collecting data from subjects. In addition, most of the frameworks focus on the protection of the individuals' privacy, confidentiality, integrity, security, authorship, and ownership. The issues of data governance, renegotiation, and data-sharing are also met in most frameworks as well. The specific data-related ethics statements from all frameworks are available in Appendix A.

Table 2.7 Data-related ethics competence statements according to the data-related ethics frameworks

Competence statement	Data-ethics framework [a]					
	1	2	3	4	5	6
Protect individuals' data privacy, confidentiality, integrity, and security	X	X	X	X		
Understand authorship, ownership, data access (governance), re-negotiation and data- sharing		X	X		X	X
Clarify who is responsible for storage, management, and access to data			X			
Respect the individuals to whom the data pertains, organizations that originate the data, organizations that aggregate the data, and those that might regulate the data					X	
Use of informed consent (notice and transparency, authentication of subjects, use limitations, anonymization, benefits)	X	X	X	X	X	X
Individuals must be made aware of when personal information about them is collected, by whom, and for what purpose			X			
Justify the primary purpose/benefits for using this data						X
Ethical data use should be done with an expectation of tangible benefit– define the usefulness or merit that comes from solving the problem					X	
Understand the limitations of the data, data source(s), and how they are being mitigated				X		

[a] [1] Demchenko and Belloum (2017); [2] Zook et al. (2017); [3] Clark et al. (2015); [4] Hancock (2018); [5] IAF (2015); [6] ODI (2017)

2.4 Educational Data Literacy Professional Development and University Courses

2.4.1 Educational Data Literacy Courses: Environmental Scan

This section presents an environmental scan on existing professional development and university courses and/or programs on the topic of educational data literacy. The objective of this section is to identify professional development or university courses and/or programs related to educational data literacy that can be considered relevant and useful to identify key EDL-related learning objectives and, thus, targeted EDL competences.

The presented courses were retrieved after an extensive search of the keywords "educational data" and "learning analytics" in:

(a) MOOC providers:

- EdX (https://www.edx.org/).
- Udemy (https://www.udemy.com/).
- Udacity (https://www.udacity.com/).
- Coursera (https://www.coursera.org/).
- FutureLearn https://www.futurelearn.com/).
- Canvas Network (https://www.canvas.net/).
- Stanford Lagunita (https://lagunita.stanford.edu/).
- Miríadax (https://miriadax.net/home).
- SWAYAM (https://swayam.gov.in/explorer).

(b) MOOC aggregators:

- mooc-list.com (https://www.mooc-list.com/),
- classcentral.com (https://www.classcentral.com/),
- EMMA—European Multiple MOOC Aggregator (https://platform.europeanmoocs.eu/).
- EPALE—Electronic Platform for Adult Learning in Europe (https://epale.ec.europa.eu/en).

(c) Google search.

The time period of the search was from 2010 to 2019. The search was performed from 19 to 23 of September 2019.

Criteria for inclusion were that the courses should be:

- In English.
- Accessible online.
- Meet the topic of the study.

We excluded courses that were related to data analytics in other contexts apart from education and courses related to digital literacy and other educational competences apart from educational data literacy.

All courses were characterized according to the following fields:

- Title of the course
- Type of course
- Targeted audience
- Offered by
- Means of delivery
- Cost
- Duration
- Expected workload to study the course
- Learning objectives
- Link with the existing EDL competence framework
- Structure
- Method of assessment

We recognize that there could be universities and/or professional development courses offered that are not included in this search as they are not open.

The key investigation steps in our environmental scan were:

1. Identify the main EDL-related learning objectives that are identified in the selected courses.
2. Recognize EDL competences related to these learning objectives and identify their main EDL competence dimensions?

Taking into account the selection criteria of the environmental scan, we identified *18 university/professional development courses*, most of which are related to fundamentals of learning analytics concepts and usage, with a duration of 5 weeks on average. None of them is explicitly linked to an existing EDL competence framework, not even the five professional development courses (see Appendix B.1 for the courses' overview). Table 2.8 summarizes the identified educational data literacy courses.

Thirteen of the courses are university courses, eight of which are offered by EdX. Four courses have fees for attending, while 14 courses are free. Appendix B.2 gathers the EDL-related learning objectives that are identified in the selected courses, as reported in their syllabus. Then, these learning objectives are processed and grouped to reveal the EDL-related competences implied and their dimensions. Table 2.9 presents these results.

As seen from this table, among the objectives of these courses are (a) to understand and use data effectively, (b) to efficiently collect educational data and metadata from a wide range of data sources for future analyses and to manipulate these educational data sets that capture the learning experience, (c) to apply data processing methods and conduct (basic) data wrangling, (d) to apply data visualization methods and analyses, (e) to address validity issues and statistics interpretations, (f)

Table 2.8 EDL-related courses

ID	Title	Type	Offered by	Cost
[1]	Data literacy 01	Professional Development course	Art of educating	Fees are applied
[2]	Analytics for the classroom teacher	University course	EdX	Free (open)—verified certificate (paid)
[3]	Learning analytics fundamentals	University course	EdX	Free (open)—verified certificate (paid)
[4]	Big data and education	University course	EdX	Free (open)—verified certificate (paid)
[5]	Data, analytics and learning	University course	EdX	Free
[6]	Practical learning analytics	University course	EdX	Free
[7]	Data literacy for school teachers—EDPZ6012	University course	University of Sydney	Fees are applied
[8]	Advancing computational and data literacy skills schools for life scientists	Professional Development course	National History Museum	Fees are applied
[9]	Introduction to data wise: A collaborative process to Improve Learning & Teaching	University course	EdX	Free (open)—verified certificate (paid)
[10]	Using data to provide personalized student support	University course	EdX	Free (open)—verified certificate (paid)
[11]	Trusted learning analytics	University course	Open Universiteit Netherlands (*OUNL*) via OpenEdX	Free
[12]	Learning analytics in higher education	University course	EdX	Free (open)—verified certificate (paid)
[13]	Learning analytics unraveled	University course	Maastricht university	Free
[14]	Analytics in course design: Leveraging canvas data (HE)	Professional Development course	Canvas	Free
[15]	NOC: Introduction to learning analytics	University course	IIT Bombay via NPTEL	Free
[16]	Learning analytics and knowledge LAK13	Professional Development course	Canvas	Free
[17]	Using data to improve student outcomes	Professional Development course	FutureLearn	Free (open)—verified certificate (paid)
[18]	Learning analytics: Process and theory	University course	The University of Edinburgh	Fees are applied

Table 2.9 EDL-related competences identified from the learning objectives of EDL-related courses

EDL competences: dimensions and statements	[1]	[2]	[3]	[4]	[5]	[6]	[7]	[8]	[9]	[10]	[11]	[12]	[13]	[14]	[15]	[16]	[17]	[18]
D1. Educational data collection: D1.a recognize different types of educational data D1.b identify educational data sources D1.c be able to apply data limitations and quality measures	x							x	x	x				x	x	x	x	
D2. Data management: D2.a apply data processing methods (data cleaning, wrangling, tidying) D2.b apply data organization methods D2.c apply data preservation methods	x		x				x			x				x	x			
D3. Data analysis: D3.a data analysis (educational data mining) D3.b data visualization		x	x	x		x		x		x				x	x	x	x	

(continued)

Table 2.9 (continued)

EDL competences: dimensions and statements	[1]	[2]	[3]	[4]	[5]	[6]	[7]	[8]	[9]	[10]	[11]	[12]	[13]	[14]	[15]	[16]	[17]	[18]
D4. Data comprehension and interpretation: D4.a data properties, data errors, data discrepancies D4.b statistics interpretation D4.c insights interpretation from data analysis D4.d interpret implications to instruction										x	x			x			x	
D5. Data application: D5.a evaluate and revise instruction D5.b support data-driven decision-making. D5.c support personalized learning	x	x		x	x	x	x		x	x				x	x	x	x	x
D6. Data ethics: D6.a informed consent D6.b data privacy and security D6.c authorship, ownership		x									x	x		x	x	x		
D7. Data literacy	x	x					x	x	x									

(continued)

Table 2.9 (continued)

EDL competences: dimensions and statements	[1]	[2]	[3]	[4]	[5]	[6]	[7]	[8]	[9]	[10]	[11]	[12]	[13]	[14]	[15]	[16]	[17]	[18]
D8. Using learning analytics: D8.a descriptive LA D8.b predictive LA D8.c prescriptive LA		x	x		x	x					x	x	x		x	x		x
D9. Applying frameworks for learning analytics: D9.a SHEILA framework.												x						
D10. Use of tools: D10.a R in RStudio/ tableau D10.b Jupiter notebooks D10.c Rapidminer D10.d Gephi (for visualization) D10.e LightSIDE (for text analysis)			x	x	x		x								x	x		
D11. Leveraging platform data: D11.a Moodle D11.b canvas		x											x					

to employ teaching analytics to analyze the lesson plans, (g) to inform teaching and learning decisions and to deploy personalized support actions for the students, (h) to use data-driven methods to answer practical educational questions, (i) to reflect on the teaching practice by combining insights from both teaching and learning analytics, and (j) to raise ethics and privacy considerations. It should be noted that none of the identified courses was directly linked to any of the existing EDC CFs.

Chapter 3
The Learn2Analyse Educational Data Literacy Competence Profile

Abstract This chapter presents a working definition of educational data literacy (EDL) for digital education professionals. This definition was synthesized from seven core existing EDL definitions and five EDL competence frameworks. It has been developed to focus on the competence set which is required to be possessed by educators to give meaning to and act upon educational data from different sources, with the aim of continuously improving the teaching, learning, and assessment process, in an ethical aspect. This chapter also presents the synthesis of the Learn2Analyse Educational Data Literacy Competence Profile (L2A-EDL-CP), which was initially developed based on the analysis of Chap. 2, and it was validated through an expert-based questionnaire-driven online survey with 210 experts from higher education institutes and e-learning industry enterprises. The proposed revised validated competence framework consists of 6 competence dimensions and 17 competence statements which aim to describe these dimensions targeting the educational data literacy needs of digital education professionals.

Keywords Educational data literacy · Educational data analytics · Teaching and learning analytics · Online and blended learning · Competence profiles · Teacher education and professional development

3.1 Scope

The scope of this chapter is to present a working definition of EDL for digital education professionals, as well as the synthesis of the Learn2Analyse Educational Data Literacy Competence Profile, which was initially developed based on the analysis of Chap. 2, and it was validated through an expert-based questionnaire-driven online survey with 210 experts from higher education institutes and e-learning industry enterprises (Papamitsiou et al., 2021). The proposed revised validated competence framework consists of 6 competence *dimensions* and 17 competence *statements* which aim to describe these dimensions targeting the educational data literacy needs of digital education professionals.

D. Sampson et al., *Educational Data Literacy*, Advances in Analytics for Learning and Teaching, https://doi.org/10.1007/978-3-031-11705-3_3

3.2 A Working Definition of Educational Data Literacy

Based on the analysis of the educational data literacy conceptual definitions in Sect. 2.2, effective educational data use at all levels requires going beyond understanding the educational data and their properties to making meaningful and actionable interpretations of these data. In other words, data literate educators must interpret the educational data in a meaningful manner and translate these data into actions that inform instruction, to improve teaching and learning; similarly, data-literate educational leaders must adopt a data-driven evidence analysis perspective to improve the overall school performance. As Mandinach and Gummer (2016) pointed out, the decisions that educators need to use educational data to inform are multiple and diverse, and educational data literacy is tailored to the specific use (context-aware). An important aspect in this process, highlighted in the literature, is the ethical considerations that should be consistent throughout all phases of data manipulations.

When it comes to determining educational data literacy for digital education professionals and educators, at large, the previous definitions require additional particularization, and the corresponding frameworks need to be adjusted accordingly. We argue that educational data literacy for these targeted roles covers much more than technical skills. As such, in the Learn2Analyze initiative, educational data literacy can be synopsized as:

> *The ability to collect, manage, analyze, comprehend, interpret, and apply educational data in an ethical, meaningful, and critical manner.*

This definition was *synthesized from the seven core existing EDL definitions and the five EDL competence frameworks*. It has been developed to *focus on the competence set* which is required to be possessed by educators to give meaning to and act upon educational data from different sources, with the aim of continuously improving the teaching, learning, and assessment process, in an ethical aspect. Furthermore, this brief definition uses *six loaded terms*, which we use as the *top level of a hierarchy of competences* and tasks that comprise EDL: collect, manage, analyze, comprehend and interpret, apply, and data ethics.

As such, the working definition for educational data literacy with a focus on ID and eTUT of online and blended (*K-12*, professional development, and/or higher education) courses pertains to the ethical, systematic, and iterative collection, management, analysis, comprehension, and interpretation of educational data to determine actionable decisions and policy in online/blended learning settings. As a context-aware process, EDL is an inquiry cycle that involves (a) data collection (e.g., location, discovery, and access) and management (e.g., cleaning, organization, and preservation) (*data level*); (b) data analysis (e.g., coding, analytics extraction, reporting on them), comprehension, and interpretation (e.g., transforming the information from analytics into usable knowledge) (*data analytics level*); and (c) data application (e.g., deciding adaptations, providing feedback) (*acting upon data level*) to be used to inform instructional design of online/blended courses (ID) and to inform students' guidance support during online/blended courses (eTUT). In the beginning of the process, identifying the objectives/problems and setting a purpose

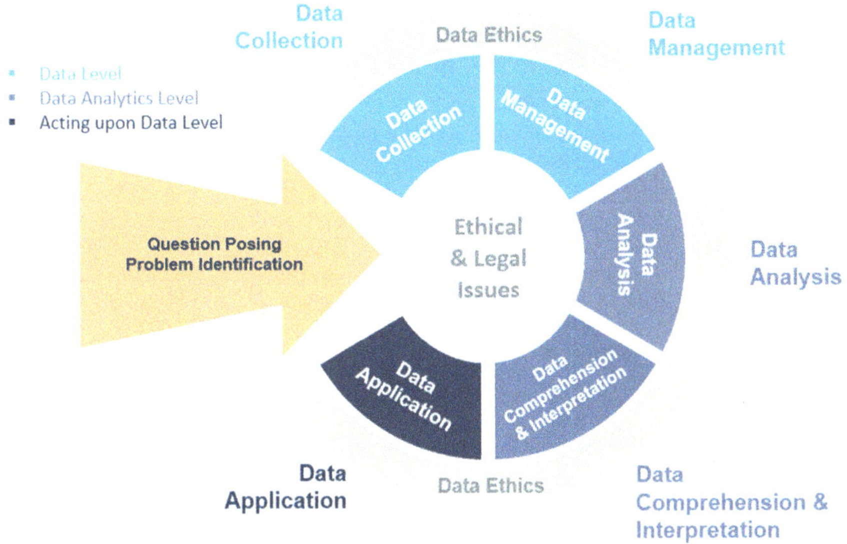

Fig. 3.1 The Learn2Analyze EDL conceptual definition

are required. In the broader definition of EDL and throughout the inquiry cycle, ethical and legal aspects catalyze the context-aware process cross-phase. This process is synopsized in Fig. 3.1.

3.3   Educational Data Literacy Competence Dimensions

Based on the analysis of the existing EDL competence frameworks presented in Sect. 2.3 and in agreement with the above-proposed L2A EDL conceptual definition, we propose (i) two broader EDL competence dimensions and (ii) six highly data-oriented, fine-grained EDL competence dimensions in our L2A EDL competence framework. The identified competence dimensions are briefly described in Tables 3.1 and 3.2.

3.4   Synthesis of Initial Learn2Analyse Educational Data Literacy Competence Profile

Based on the above analysis, we developed an initial *Educational Data Literacy Competence Profile* for Digital Education professionals, which is summarized in Table 3.3. This competence profile consists of *6* competence *dimensions* and *21* competence *statements* which aim to describe these dimensions.

Table 3.1 Generic dimensions of the Learn2Analyze EDL Competence Framework

Generic EDL competence dimension	Short description	Citing frameworks
Ethical/legal issues	Considering ethical restrictions and concerns, including security, confidentiality, privacy, informed consent, anonymity of peoples' data	Data Quality Campaign (2014); Wolff et al. (2016)
Problem identification	Formulating hypotheses about students' learning needs, asking questions that can be researched using data, aligning learning goals with available data, as well as articulating and highlighting problems with a topic area, an aspect of instruction, or the curriculum	Means et al. (2011); Mandinach and Gummer (2016), Wolff et al. (2016)

Table 3.2 Data-related dimensions of the Learn2Analyze EDL Competence Framework

Educational data-related competence dimension	Short description	Citing frameworks
Data collection	Determining fit-for-purpose data, finding and accessing the right data, collecting qualitative and quantitative data from multiple sources, using methods such as conducting interviews, creating surveys, making observations and taking measurements, etc.	All except Love (2012); Mandinach and Gummer (2013, 2016)
Data management	Organizing, cleaning, and preserving data, converting data (from format to format), creating and utilizing metadata, curating data, etc.	Ridsdale et al. (2015); Wolff et al. (2016); Marsh (2012); Prado and Marzal (2013)
Data analysis	Understanding the measurement error, the influence of sample size on the ability to generalize, understanding uses of data quality (e.g., accuracy, completeness), etc.	Love (2012); North Carolina Department of Public Instruction (2013); Wolff et al. (2016); Marsh (2012)
Data comprehension/ interpretation	Reading and understanding charts, tables, and graphs, using data displays and representations, assessing patterns and trends, moving fluently between alternative data representations, probing for causality, understanding statistics and psychometrics, etc.	All except Love (2012); Ridsdale et al. (2015)
Data application	Making instructional adjustments, applying the knowledge produced to create the appropriate environment and applying the right strategy and plan to facilitate learning, adjusting practices using student performance data, integrating data use with curriculum instruction and assessment, evaluate intervention, etc.	All

Table 3.3 Initial L2A Educational Data Literacy competence profile

L2A EDL Competence dimension	L2A EDL Competence statements
1. Data collection	1.1 Know where to find the right data/data sources
	1.2 Know how to obtain/access data
	1.3 Understand data quality and limitations (e.g., accuracy, completeness)
2. Data management	2.1 Identify the technologies to preserve data
	2.2 Know and apply data manipulation methods
	2.3 Know and apply data curation and data reuse methods
	2.4 Understand data description (metadata)
3. Data analysis	3.1 Know and apply the basic data analysis methods
	3.2 Understand and apply the basic data analysis process steps
	3.3 Understand and apply the basic data presentation methods
4. Data comprehension and interpretation	4.1 Understand data (e.g., measurement error, discrepancies within data, key take away points)
	4.2 Understand statistics
	4.3 Know how to interpret data (e.g., explanations of patterns, identification of hypotheses, connection of multiple observations)
	4.4 Generate potential connections to instruction
	4.5 Make decisions based on data
5. Data application	5.1 Use data to inform instruction
	5.2 Know how to share and cite data
	5.3 Evaluate the data-driven intervention
6. Data ethics	6.1 Explain the use of informed consent
	6.2 Know how to protect individuals' data privacy, confidentiality, integrity, and security
	6.3 Understand authorship, ownership, data access (governance), renegotiation, and data-sharing

3.5   Experts' Validation of the Initial L2A Educational Data Literacy Competence Profile

In order to validate the initial L2A-EDL-CP and identify areas of possible improvement, *an expert-based questionnaire-driven online survey* was designed and implemented, within the European context (and beyond, to have eventually a global impact and reach out), with *210 experts* from *higher education institutes* and *e-learning industry enterprises*. The detailed validation process is presented in the open access paper "Towards an educational data literacy framework: enhancing the profiles of instructional designers and e-tutors of online and blended courses with new competences" (Papamitsiou et al., 2021).

This survey was conducted between 1st September and 15th October 2018. The core issue for investigation in this survey was:

- Is the proposed *Educational Data Literacy (EDL) Competence Profile (CP)* framework (including *6 dimensions* and *21 statements*) appropriate to describe the essential competences of digital education professionals?

The core question was investigated on the following dimensions:

- If the proposed statements *address well* the corresponding EDL competence dimensions.
- If the proposed statements *are important for* the EDL competences of digital education professionals.
- If the proposed statements *are well written.*
- Recommendations for *alternative and/or additional statements* for the EDL competence dimensions.

Extending the quantitative and qualitative analyses and recommendations as induced by the *expert-based questionnaire-driven online survey*, the L2A-EDL-CP has been revised accordingly. The changes applied are synopsized as follows:

1. A consistent 3 level description "know—understand—be able to apply," corresponding to different levels of expertise (basic, advanced, expert or novice, experienced, expert), is employed to replace "know how," "know and apply," "understand," etc. for each competence statement.
2. A widely accepted definition of the unclear/confusing term and/or specific examples that clarify the term are provided in parenthesis, where needed, next to the competence statement.
3. For the terms used in the statements of the dimensions data collection (D1), data management (D2), data analysis (D3), data comprehension (D4), as well as data ethics (D6), definitions from standard data science textbooks are employed (Tattar et al., 2017; Berson & Dubov, 2010; Cady, 2017).

As a result, the following modifications were made:

- S1-D1 (*"Know where to find the right data/data sources"*) of EDL-CP-v1 has been merged with S2-D1 (*"know how to obtain/access data"*) and the new statement has been rewritten as S1-D1 (*"know-understand-be able to obtain, access, and gather the appropriate data and/or data sources"*) of EDL-CP-v2 in order to be consistent with the 3 level description of the different levels of expertise and because the experts identified/reported an overlap between the previous two.
- S3-D1 (*"Understand data quality and limitations (e.g., accuracy, completeness)"*) of EDL-CP-v1 has become S2-D1 (*"Know-understand-be able to apply data limitations and quality measures (e.g., validity, reliability, biases in the data, difficulty in collection, accuracy, completeness)"*) of EDL-CP-v2 in order to be consistent with the 3 level description of the different levels of expertise, as well as because S2-D1 was merged with S1-D1 of EDL-CP-v1 in the previous step.
- S1-D2 (*"Identify the technologies to preserve data"*) of EDL-CP-v1 has been reordered in EDL-CP-v2, and it has become S4-D2, in order to comply with the widely accepted definition of the data management cycle. Furthermore, it has

been rewritten as *"know-understand-be able to apply the technologies to preserve data (i.e., store, persist, maintain, backup data), e.g., storage mediums/ services, tools, mechanisms)"* to be consistent with the 3 level description of the different levels of expertise, as well as because it was identified as a statement on the boundary or revision (from the quantitative analysis).

- S2-D2 (*"Know and apply data manipulation methods"*) of EDL-CP-v1 has been re-ordered in EDL-CP-v2, and it has become S1-D2, in order to comply with the widely accepted definition of the data management cycle. It has also been rewritten as *"know-understand-be able to apply data processing and handling methods (i.e., methods for cleaning and changing data to make it more organized—e.g., deduplication, data structuring,"* according to the suggestions of the experts.

- S3-D2 (*"Know and apply data curation and data reuse methods"*) of EDL-CP-v1 has been rewritten as S3-D2 (*"Know-understand-be able to apply data curation processes (i.e., to ensure that data is reliably retrievable for future reuse, and to determine what data is worth saving and for how long)"*) in EDL-CP-v2, to be consistent with the 3 level description of the different levels of expertise.

- S4-D2 (*"Understand Data Description (Metadata)"*) of EDL-CP-v1 has been re-ordered as S2-D2 in EDL-CP-v2 to comply with the widely accepted definition of the data management cycle, and it has been rewritten as *"Know-understand-be able to apply data description (i.e., metadata),"* to be consistent with the 3 level description of the different levels of expertise.

- S1-D3 (*"Know and apply the basic data analysis methods"*) and S2-D3 (*"Understand and apply the basic data analysis process steps"*) of EDL-CP-v1 have been merged and rewritten as S1-D3 (*"Know-understand-be able to apply data analysis and modeling methods (e.g., application of descriptive statistics, exploratory data analysis, data mining)"*) in EDL-CP-v2, because the experts identified and reported significant overlap between the previous two and in order to be consistent with the 3 level description of the different levels of expertise.

- S3-D3 (*"Understand and apply the basic data presentation methods"*) of EDL-CP-v1 has become S2-D3 (*"Know-understand-be able to apply data presentation methods (e.g., pictorial visualization of the data by using graphs, charts, maps, and other data forms like textual or tabular representations)"*) of EDL-CP-v2, after the merging of S1-D3 and S2-D3 in the previous step. Furthermore, the statement has been rewritten to be consistent with the 3 level description of expertise, and specific examples have been added to clarify the statement.

- S1-D4 (*"Understand data (e.g., measurement error, discrepancies within data, key take-away points)"*) of EDL-CP-v1 has been rewritten as S1-D4 (*"Know-understand-be able to interpret data properties (e.g., measurement error, outliers, discrepancies within data, key take-away points, data dependencies)"*) in EDL-CP-v2, as a result of the quantitative analysis, and according to the suggestions of the experts, using additional examples to clarify the statement.

- S2-D4 (*"Understand statistics"*) of EDL-CP-v1 has been rewritten as S2-D2 (*"Know-understand-be able to interpret statistics commonly used with educational data (e.g., randomness, central tendencies, mean, standard deviation, significance)"*) in EDL-CP-v2, as a result of the quantitative analysis, in order to be consistent with the 3 level description of the different levels of expertise and according to the suggestions of the experts, using additional examples to clarify the statement.

- S3-D4 (*"Know how to interpret data (e.g., explanations of patterns, identification of hypotheses, connection of multiple observations)"*) of EDL-CP-v1 has been rewritten as S3-D4 (*"Know-understand-be able to interpret insights from data analysis (e.g., explanations of patterns, identification of hypotheses, connection of multiple observations, underlying trends)"*) in EDL-CP-v2, in order to be consistent with the 3 level description of the different levels of expertise and according to the suggestions of the experts.
- S4-D4 (*"Generate potential connections to instruction"*) of EDL-CP-v1 has been revised and rewritten as S4-D4 (*"Be able to elicit potential implications/ links of the data analysis insights to instruction"*) in EDL-CP-v2, as a result of the quantitative analysis, according to the suggestions of the experts.
- S5-D4 (*"Make decisions based on data"*) of EDL-CP-v1 has been removed in the revised EDL-CP-v2 according to the suggestions of the experts, because an overlap with D5 was identified and reported.
- S1-D5 (*"Use data to inform instruction"*) of EDL-CP-v1 has been rewritten as S1-D5 (*"Know-understand-be able to use data analysis results to make decisions to revise instruction"*) in EDL-CP-v2, in order to be consistent with the 3 level description of the different levels of expertise, to include S5-D4 of EDL-CP-v1 (as explained in the previous step) and according to the suggestions of the experts.
- S2-D5 (*"Know how to share and cite data"*) of EDL-CP-v1 has been removed in the revised EDL-CP-v2 because the qualitative analysis revealed an overlap with S3-D6 (*"Understand authorship, ownership, data access (governance), renegotiation, and data-sharing"*) of EDL-CP-v1. Furthermore, since D6 is a transversal dimension, it was decided to keep this statement as part of D6 in the revised EDL-CP-v2.
- S3-D5 (*"Evaluate the data-driven intervention"*) of EDL-CP-v1 has been reordered as S2-D5 (*"Be able to evaluate the data-driven revision of instruction"*) in EDL-CP-v2, after the removal of S2-D5, as explained in the previous step.
- S1-D6 (*"Explain the use of informed consent"*) of EDL-CP-v1 has been rewritten as S1-D6 (*"Know-understand-be able to use the informed consent"*) in EDL-CP-v2, in order to be consistent with the 3 level description of the different levels of expertise.
- S2-D6 (*"Know how to protect individuals' data privacy, confidentiality, integrity, and security"*) of EDL-CP-v1 has been rewritten as S2-D6 (*"Know-understand-be able to protect individuals' data privacy, confidentiality, integrity, and security"*) in EDL-CP-v2, in order to be consistent with the 3 level description of the different levels of expertise.
- S3-D6 (*"Understand authorship, ownership, data access (governance), renegotiation, and data-sharing"*) of EDL-CP-v1 has been rewritten as S3-D6 (*"Know-understand-be able to apply authorship, ownership, data access (governance),*

renegotiation, and data-sharing") in EDL-CP-v2, in order to be consistent with the 3 level description of the different levels of expertise.

The revised validated L2A-EDL-CP (Competence Dimensions and Competence Statements per Dimension) is demonstrated in Table 3.4.

Table 3.4 Revised validated EDL CP Framework

L2A EDL Competence dimension	L2A EDL Competence statements
1. Data collection	1.1 Know-understand-be able to obtain, access, and gather the appropriate data and/or data sources
	1.2 Know-understand-be able to apply data limitations and quality measures (e.g., validity, reliability, biases in the data, difficulty in collection, accuracy, completeness)
2. Data management	2.1 Know-understand-be able to apply data processing and handling methods (i.e., methods for cleaning and changing data to make it more organized – e.g., deduplication, data structuring)
	2.2 Know-understand-be able to apply data description (i.e., metadata)
	2.3 Know-understand-be able to apply data curation processes (i.e., to ensure that data is reliably retrievable for future reuse, and to determine what data is worth saving and for how long)
	2.4 Know-understand-be able to apply the technologies to preserve data (i.e., store, persist, maintain, backup data), e.g., storage mediums/ services, tools, mechanisms
3. Data analysis	3.1 Know-understand-be able to apply data analysis and modelling methods (e.g., textual or tabular representations)
	3.2 Know-understand-be able to apply data presentation methods (e.g., pictorial visualization of the data by using graphs, charts, maps, and other data forms like textual or tabular representations)
4. Data comprehension and interpretation	4.1 Know-understand-be able to interpret data properties (e.g., measurement error, outliers, discrepancies within data, key take-away points, data dependencies)
	4.2 Know-understand-be able to interpret statistics commonly used with educational data (e.g., randomness, central tendencies, mean, standard deviation, significance)
	4.3 Know-understand-be able to interpret insights from data analysis (e.g., explanations of patterns, identification of hypotheses, connection of multiple observations, underlying trends)
	4.4 Be able to elicit potential implications/links of the data analysis insights to instruction
5. Data application	5.1 Know-understand-be able to use data analysis results to make decisions to revise instruction
	5.2 Be able to evaluate the data-driven revision of instruction
6. Data ethics	6.1 Know-understand-be able to use informed consent
	6.2 Know-understand-be able to protect individuals' data privacy, confidentiality, integrity, and security
	6.3 Know-understand-be able to apply authorship, ownership, data access (governance), renegotiation, and data-sharing

Chapter 4
Learn2Analyse Educational Data Literacy Competence Profile: From Theory to Practice

Abstract This chapter presents the exemplary learning outcomes for the two-dimensional Educational Data Literacy Competence Profile (EDL-CP) framework and the use-case examples for indicative target groups of the EDL-CP. The exemplary learning outcomes express what individuals should know, understand, and be able to do at the end of a learning process focusing on a specific dimension/statement of the L2A-EDL-CP framework. The L2A use-case examples focusing on each dimension/statement of the L2A-EDL-CP framework provide insights about how competence may be demonstrated in a specific context. In particular, three use-case examples have been developed: (a) instructional designer in industry context, (b) e-trainer in higher education context, and (c) teacher in K-12 context. Each use-case example includes a background story and exemplary activities in correspondence with the L2A-EDL-CP dimensions, statements, as well as specific learning outcomes.

Keywords Educational data literacy · Educational data analytics · Teaching and learning analytics · Online and blended learning · Competence profiles · Teacher education and professional development

4.1 Scope

The scope of this chapter is to present the exemplary learning outcomes for the two-dimensional L2A-EDL-CP framework and the use-case examples for indicative target groups of the L2A-EDL-CP, namely, instructional designers, e-trainers, and K-12 teachers.

4.2   Exemplary Learning Outcomes

The exemplary learning outcomes express what individuals should know, understand, and be able to do at the end of a learning process focusing on a specific dimension/statement of the EDL-CP framework. Hence, the exemplary learning outcomes need to be differentiated for different target groups of learners, i.e., instructional designers, e-trainers, or teachers in K-12. Table 4.1 presents the exemplary learning outcomes for the EDL-CP framework for instructional designers and e-trainers. Three levels of learning outcomes are differentiated (Anderson et al., 2001): (a) know, (b) understand, (c) be able to.

4.3   Use-Case Examples for Selected Target Groups

In general, a use-case is defined as a specific situation in which a service or product could potentially be used. The L2A use-case examples focusing on each dimension/statement of the L2A-EDL-CP framework provide insights about how competence may be demonstrated in a specific context. In particular, three use-case examples have been developed: (a) instructional designer in industry context, (b) e-trainer in higher education context, and (c) teacher in K-12 context. Each use-case example includes a background story and exemplary activities in correspondence with the L2A-EDL-CP dimensions, statements, as well as specific learning outcomes.

4.3.1   Use-Case Example for Instructional Designer in Industry Context

4.3.1.1   Background Story for Instructional Designer Use-Case

David works as an instructional designer for a training consulting company. The company provides a wide range of services, from tailor-made course offerings (face2face classroom based, blended learning, and online, including massive open online courses—MOOCs) to educational technology consulting. Karen, his manager, has put David in charge of a new innovative project: an important client—a global IT company—aims to implement a learning analytics solution for their internal and external online course programs. While the client company has strong expertise in data mining and analytics, they need to have some external support from pedagogical experts on using educational data for redesigning their online courses. So, David is hired to lead the "data-driven course design" initiative at the client's site. As a pilot project within this initiative, David coordinates the redesign of a MOOC on IT management. This course primarily serves as a marketing tool for the IT company, and it has had a large participant base with high enrolment numbers over recent years. However, participant engagement and completion rates were not satisfactory overall. Thus, the client wants to implement a number of pedagogical

Table 4.1 Exemplary learning outcomes for the final revised validated L2A-EDL-CP

L2A-EDL-CP dimension	L2A-EDL-CP statement	Level of learning outcome	Exemplary learning outcome	
			The instructional designer will …	The e-trainer will …
1. Data collection	1.1	Know	List one or more data sources that support building pedagogically sound online blended courses	List one or more ways to access educational process data for the use in online blended courses
		Understand	Differentiate between different sources of educational data with regard to accessibility	Same
		Be able to	Apply methods and technologies to access educational data in an efficient and timely manner	Same
	1.2	Know	Name different indicators of data quality relevant to working with educational data	Same
		Understand	Explain different indicators of data quality and their meaning when working with educational data sets	Same
		Be able to	Review educational data on the basis of different quality indicators	Same

(continued)

Table 4.1 (continued)

2. Data management	2.1	Know	Describe methods for cleaning and organizing educational data sets	Same
		Understand	Outline an organized structure for educational data sets suitable for further analysis	Same
		Be able to	Apply data cleaning and organizing methods to a given set of raw educational product data	Apply data cleaning and organizing methods to a given set of raw educational process data
	2.2	Know	List appropriate metadata descriptors for educational data sets	Same
		Understand	Describe the differences and commonalities of two or more sets of educational data on the basis of their metadata	Same
		Be able to	Develop metadata descriptions for raw educational data	Same
	2.3	Know	Name the steps of a generic data curation process for educational data sets	Same
		Understand	Determine what educational data has to be saved for future reuse	Same
		Be able to	Apply methods to organize and integrate educational data collected from various sources	Same
	2.4	Know	List different tools and mechanisms to preserve educational data	Same
		Understand	Evaluate different tools and mechanisms to preserve educational data and explain their (dis-)advantages	Same
		Be able to	Develop and execute a reliable data backup plan for persistent storage of educational data	Same

(continued)

Table 4.1 (continued)

3. Data analysis	3.1	Know	Name the basic data modelling methods and their outcomes with respect to educational data analysis	Same
		Understand	Explain the process of educational data mining	Same
		Be able to	Apply the basic data analysis and modelling methods to a given set of educational product data	Apply the basic data analysis and modelling methods to a given set of educational process data
	3.2	Know	Name various approaches for the (re)presentation of educational data	Same
		Understand	Differentiate between the various forms of visualization and representation of educational data with respect to scope, strengths and weaknesses	Same
		Be able to	Illustrate the process of data presentation by applying one presentation method to a given data analytics problem involving educational product data	Illustrate the process of data presentation by applying one presentation method to a given data analytics problem involving educational process data

(continued)

4. Data comprehension and interpretation	4.1	Know	Name the most important data properties within educational data sets	Same
		Understand	Explain the influence of data properties like outliers and missing values on the statistical analysis of educational data	Same
		Be able to	Characterize a given set of educational product data with respect to data properties	Characterize a given set of educational process data with respect to data properties
	4.2	Know	Name and differentiate the most commonly used statistics for educational data analysis	Same
		Understand	Explain the concept of significance in the context of educational data analysis	Same
		Be able to	Interpret the basic measures of central tendency and variation for a given set of educational product data	Interpret the basic measures of central tendency and variation for a given set of educational process data
	4.3	Know	Sketch possible insights from the analysis of a set of educational product data	Sketch possible insights from the analysis of a set of educational process data
		Understand	Identify trends and hypotheses from a given set of educational data	Same
		Be able to	Evaluate the scope and appropriateness of interpretations based on educational data analysis	Same
	4.4	Know	Clearly communicate the links from data analysis insights to instructional design	Clearly communicate the links from data analysis insights to instructional processes
		Understand	Develop possible instructional design alternatives based on findings	Develop possible tutorial interventions based on findings
		Be able to	Infer general design principles for blended and online courses from data	Infer general tutoring principles for blended and online courses from data

Table 4.1 (continued)

5. Data application	5.1	Know	Name the areas to be improved based on the findings from educational data analysis	Same
		Understand	Design automatic prompts based on findings from data analysis	Give individual process feedback based on findings from data analysis
		Be able to	Revise course tasks and contents based on findings from data analysis	Revise the current tutoring strategy based on findings from data analysis.
	5.2	Know	Construct adequate criteria and indicators for evaluating the impact of a data-driven intervention	Same
		Understand	Conduct a methodologically sound evaluation of a data-driven intervention	Same
		Be able to	Communicate the evaluation results of the data-driven revision of instruction	Same

(continued)

Table 4.1 (continued)

6. Data ethics	6.1	Know	Explain the concept of informed consent in the context of educational data analysis	Same
		Understand	Name one or more arguments for the importance of informed consent in educational data analysis	Same
		Be able to	Link the use of informed consent in educational data analysis to data protection regulations and legal foundations	Same
	6.2	Know	Explain the notion of data privacy in the context of educational data analysis	Same
		Understand	Distinguish between different levels of data protection in educational data analysis	Same
		Be able to	Take adequate actions to protect individuals' data privacy and integrity in educational data analysis	Same
	6.3	Know	Name different concepts of data access (governance) in educational data analysis	Same
		Understand	Explain the differences between authorship and ownership when dealing with educational data	Same
		Be able to	Apply those concepts to a given educational data analysis problem correctly	Same

innovations in a redesigned version of the course, with the overarching goal of increasing learner satisfaction. It is part of David's mission to develop a strategy which is based on educational data and analytics.

4.3.1.2   Use-Case Activities for Instructional Designer in Industry Context

Table 4.2 shows the L2A-EDL-CP use-case example for the instructional designer in industry context linked to the dimensions/statements of the L2A-EDL-CP.

A short version of the use-case example for the instructional designer in industry context is represented in Fig. 4.1.

Table 4.2 Use-case examples for the instructional designer in industry context linked to the L2A-EDL-CP

Dimension	Statement	Use-case instructional designer in industry context
1. Data collection	1.1 Know—understand—be able to obtain, access, and gather the appropriate data and/or data sources	David sets up a project team on site together with some employees of the client company. As a first step in the MOOC redesign project, he tries to get an overview of the different data and data sources that could help to get an idea of learner satisfaction. Therefore, he talks to different people from the IT and the training department and compiles a list of available data and the respective systems (evaluation data, LMS performance data, HR system data, etc.). Having compiled a list of data sources, David contacts the people responsible for those sources to get permission to access and use the data. The IT manager shows him how to access the LMS to get a snapshot of learner data, and he provides additional data in a transferable file format (.Csv). David imports the data sets into his spreadsheet program.
	1.2 Know—understand—be able to apply data limitations and quality measures (e.g., validity, reliability, biases in the data, difficulty in collection, accuracy, completeness)	At a status meeting with the project team, David seeks to elucidate the scope of possible inferences and insights with respect to learner satisfaction from the available educational data. Therefore, he assesses the strengths and weaknesses of the data sets at hand with the help of different indicators of data quality. For his presentation, he researches and lists different indicators (validity, reliability, objectivity, accuracy, completeness, ease of use, etc.). In the following, David applies a number of criteria to the data sets at hand, comparing them against each other. He lists the opportunities and shortcomings of the different data sets for his presentation during the meeting.

(continued)

Table 4.2 (continued)

Dimension	Statement	Use-case instructional designer in industry context
2. Data management	2.1 Know—understand—be able to apply data processing and handling methods (i.e., methods for cleaning and changing data to make it more organized—e.g., duplication, data structuring)	David takes a closer look at the available data sets. Spotting a number of duplicates as well as incomplete sets, he soon realizes that the data needs to be cleaned and processed before further analysis can take place. He researches the standard procedures for data processing and outlines a desirable structure for the data sets at hand. He then applies some data cleaning and organizing methods to implement this structure.
	2.2 Know—understand—be able to apply data description (i.e., metadata)	With the whole "data-driven course design" initiative in mind, David thinks about how educational data sets for the analysis of learner satisfaction can be described and compared on an abstract level. Therefore, he researches some common metadata approaches and selects appropriate data descriptors (e.g., course title, education level). He then applies those descriptors to the data sets in the MOOC redesign project. As a result, he develops a complete metadata description for educational data sets that can be used throughout the whole "data-driven course design" initiative.
	2.3 Know—understand—be able to apply data curation processes (i.e., to ensure that data is reliably retrievable for future reuse and to determine what data is worth saving and for how long)	Having categorized and characterized the data sets at hand, David needs to determine how to proceed with the collected data. For an analysis of learner satisfaction, it seems to be crucial that automatically generated system data and evaluation data can be combined. After discussing this with the project team, he makes some suggestions to the client on what data need to be saved for future reuse and for how long. He then sets up a data curation process, which involves a fixed number of steps from data collection and storage to future retrieval.
	2.4 Know—understand—be able to apply the technologies to preserve data (i.e., store, persist, maintain, backup data), e.g., storage mediums/ services, tools, mechanisms	For the technical aspects of data curation, David collaborates with a member of the client's IT department who is responsible for storage and database management. They discuss the pros and cons of different technologies and services for storing educational data and then develop a reliable backup plan for building up a persistent educational data repository.

(continued)

Table 4.2 (continued)

Dimension	Statement	Use-case instructional designer in industry context
3. Data analysis	3.1 Know—understand—be able to apply data analysis and modeling methods (e.g., application of descriptive statistics, exploratory data analysis, data mining)	Having prepared and organized the different sets of educational data, David has a go at data analytics. As a first step, David conducts some basic exploratory data analysis on the evaluation data and applies the basic descriptive procedures to the items and scales dealing with motivational and emotional aspects from past MOOC evaluations. With a member of the client's data science team, he discusses the pros and cons of educational data mining. Together, they try to unveil some notable patterns in the system generated data at hand, seeking to identify possible critical incidents for learner satisfaction.
	3.2 Know—understand—be able to apply data presentation methods (e.g., pictorial visualization of the data by using graphs, charts, maps and other data forms like textual or tabular representations)	For a joint steering meeting involving the client's management, as well as Karen, David needs to prepare a presentation of his results so far. He researches a number of data visualization approaches and decides on different graphs and tables for the descriptive statistics and exploratory data analysis on learner satisfaction.

(continued)

Table 4.2 (continued)

Dimension	Statement	Use-case instructional designer in industry context
4. Data comprehension and interpretation	4.1 Know—understand—be able to interpret data properties (e.g., measurement error, outliers, discrepancies within data, key takeaway points, data dependencies)	In the steering meeting presentation, David explains the basic properties of the analyzed data sets. By the example of the items on learners' initial motivation, he explains outliers, dependencies, and the like, and he explains to his audience what these properties could mean for further data analysis, understanding, and interpretation.
	4.2 Know—understand—be able to interpret statistics commonly used with educational data (e.g., randomness, central tendencies, mean, standard deviation, significance)	In the course of the steering meeting presentation, David explains the common statistics (such as means and standard deviation) used with educational data with the help of tables and graphs. Having conducted some correlation and regression analyses to illustrate relationships between input (i.e. initial motivation) and outcome (i.e. overall satisfaction, overall performance) variables, David further explains the concept of significance testing.
	4.3 Know—understand—be able to interpret insights from data analysis (e.g., explanations of patterns, identification of hypotheses, connection of multiple observations, underlying trends)	Within the steering meeting presentation, David shows and interprets some further insights from data analysis and educational data mining. He illustrates possible patterns and trends of learner satisfaction, identifying hypotheses for further research.
	4.4 Be able to elicit potential implications/links of the data analysis insights to instruction	In the discussion section of the steering meeting presentation, David links the results to the existing instructional design and design variables mapping out some possible implications from the intended changes. He identifies a number of starting points within the course from which learner satisfaction could be increased. Later, within his project team, he works on possible design alternatives based on those insights. These alternative designs include a specific focus on learners' satisfaction and include a number of possible pedagogical interventions to improve it.

(continued)

Table 4.2 (continued)

Dimension	Statement	Use-case instructional designer in industry context
5. Data application	5.1 Know—understand—be able to use data analysis results to make decisions to revise instruction	As a result of their team effort, David writes up a report on how to redesign the MOOC on IT management based on the educational data at hand. He identifies the areas to be improved and makes clear and concrete suggestions for revised course tasks and content based on the findings from data analysis. In the outlook section of his report, he discusses the potential of automatic prompting based on learner data to increase learner satisfaction. These adaptive interventions could be implemented if the data analysis was carried out in real time and automatically as it is obligatory in a full-fledged learning analytics setting.
	5.2 Be able to evaluate the data-driven revision of instruction	Together with his project team, David develops a strategy on how to evaluate the impact of the data-driven course redesign. They define indicators and criteria for measuring developments in learner satisfaction (i.e., learner activity, time-on-task, motivational and emotional items in a formative evaluation), and they sketch a methodologically sound A/B-design (i.e., a comparison of two different design cases with different "conditions" for supporting learner satisfaction) for a quasi-experimental evaluation setting.
6. Data ethics	6.1 Know—understand—be able to use the informed consent	In the context of the "data-driven course design" initiative, David seeks to establish legal and ethics procedures. Thus, he collaborates intensively with the client's legal department and discusses the various legal topics involved. As a first result, they develop a legally compliant participant form for informed consent to be presented to and signed by each person taking part in one of the client company's online courses.
	6.2 Know—understand—be able to protect individuals' data privacy, confidentiality, integrity, and security	In the course of the discussion on legal aspects, the client company's legal experts explain to and teach David how to protect the learners' data privacy, data confidentiality, data integrity, and data security.
	6.3 Know—understand—be able to apply authorship, ownership, data access (governance), renegotiation, and data sharing	Likewise, legal concepts like authorship, ownership, data access and governance, renegotiation, and data sharing are discussed. Well equipped with this specific knowledge, David writes a quick legal analysis for the "data-driven course design" initiative.

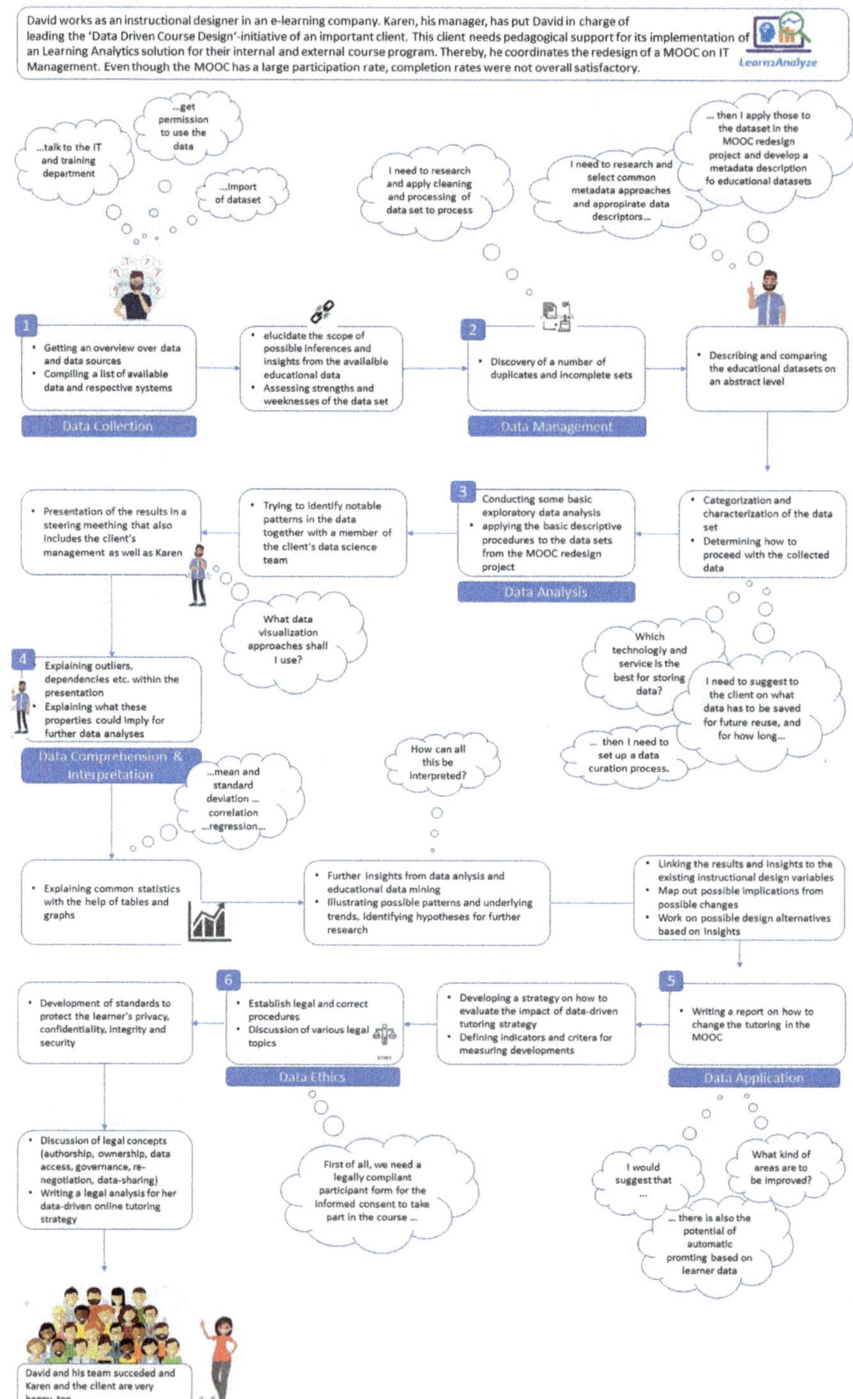

Fig. 4.1 Use-case examples for instructional designer in industry context

Table 4.3 Use-case examples for the e-trainer in higher education context linked to the L2A-EDL-CP

Dimension	Statement	Use-case e-trainer in higher education context
1. Data collection	1.1 Know—understand—be able to obtain, access, and gather the appropriate data and/or data sources	Laura has only a vague idea of the different sets of educational data linked to course completion that are being generated and processed through the MOOC and its participants. So, she tries to get a thorough overview of the data sources at hand. She gathers the relevant information from the faculty, the student service department, the MOOC provider, and the IT-department (e.g., evaluation data, MOOC performance data, enrolment data, etc.). Having compiled a list of data sources, Laura contacts the people responsible for those sources to get permission to access and use the data. The MOOC provider lets her sign a data protection consent form and grants her access to system data. She also receives a set of historical performance data in a transferable file format (.Csv) providing her initial insights into the data structure. Laura imports the data sets into her spreadsheet program.
	1.2 Know—understand—be able to apply data limitations and quality measures (e.g., validity, reliability, biases in the data, difficulty in collection, accuracy, completeness)	For a project team meeting, Laura aims to clarify how educational data might be useful for online tutoring and increasing the completion rate. Therefore, she assesses the strengths and weaknesses of the data sets at hand with the help of different indicators of data quality. For her presentation, she researches and lists different indicators (validity, reliability, objectivity, accuracy, completeness, ease of use, etc.). Next, Laura applies a number of criteria to the data sets at hand, comparing them against each other. She lists the opportunities and shortcomings of the different data sets for her presentation.

(continued)

Table 4.3 (continued)

Dimension	Statement	Use-case e-trainer in higher education context
2. Data management	2.1 Know—understand—be able to apply data processing and handling methods (i.e., methods for cleaning and changing data to make it more organized—e.g., duplication, data structuring)	Laura takes a closer look at the available data sets. Discovering a number of inconsistencies (e.g., cases related to different time zones) as well as incomplete sets, she soon realizes that the data needs to be cleaned and processed before further analysis can take place. She researches the standard procedures for data processing and outlines a desirable structure for the data sets at hand. She then applies some data cleaning and organizing methods to implement this structure.
	2.2 Know—understand—be able to apply data description (i.e., metadata)	Considering the wide range of courses also challenged by completion rate issues, Laura thinks about how educational data sets can be described and compared on a general level. Therefore, she researches some common metadata approaches and selects appropriate data descriptors (e.g., course title, student id, timestamp). She then applies those descriptors to the data sets in the MOOC redesign project. As a result, she develops a complete metadata description for educational data sets that can be used for various types of online courses.
	2.3 Know—understand—be able to apply data curation processes (i.e., to ensure that data is reliably retrievable for future reuse and to determine what data is worth saving and for how long)	Having categorized and characterized the data sets at hand, Laura needs to determine how to proceed with the collected data. She realizes that plain data on learner dropouts has to be combined with a number of direct (i.e. formative evaluation data) and indirect (i.e. time-on-task, progress) indicators to get a bigger picture of course completion. After discussing the issue within the project team, she makes some suggestions to the IT department and the MOOC provider on what data need to be saved for future reuse, how frequent, and for how long. She then sets up a data curation process, which involves a fixed number of steps from data collection and storage to future retrieval.
	2.4 Know—understand—be able to apply the technologies to preserve data (i.e., store, persist, maintain, backup data), e.g., storage mediums/ services, tools, mechanisms	For the technical aspects of data curation, Laura collaborates with a member of the university's IT department who is responsible for storage and database management. They discuss the pros and cons of different technologies and services for storing educational data and then develop a reliable backup plan for building up a persistent educational data repository.

(continued)

Table 4.3 (continued)

Dimension	Statement	Use-case e-trainer in higher education context
3. Data analysis	3.1 Know—understand—be able to apply data analysis and modeling methods (e.g., application of descriptive statistics, exploratory data analysis, data mining)	Having prepared and organized the different sets of educational data, Laura has a go at data analytics. As a first step, Laura conducts some basic exploratory data analysis with the more straightforward data sets from the MOOC provider. She generates some descriptive statistics on dropout numbers related to different course chapters. An additional member of the project team who is an expert in learning analytics tells her about the pros and cons of educational data mining. Together, they try to identify some emergent patterns in the more complex sets of system data with regard to course completion (e.g., clusters of possible early dropouts).
	3.2 Know—understand—be able to apply data presentation methods (e.g., pictorial visualization of the data by using graphs, charts, maps, and other data forms like textual or tabular representations)	For a larger steering meeting involving Prof. Chang as well as the head of the department, Laura has to prepare a presentation of her results so far. She researches a number of data visualization approaches and decides on different graphs and tables for the descriptive statistics and the results of the exploratory data analysis on dropouts and completion.

(continued)

Table 4.3 (continued)

Dimension	Statement	Use-case e-trainer in higher education context
4. Data comprehension and interpretation	4.1 Know—understand—be able to interpret data properties (e.g., measurement error, outliers, discrepancies within data, key takeaway points, data dependencies)	In the steering meeting presentation, Laura explains the basic properties of the analyzed data sets. Using the example of dropouts per course chapter, she explains outliers, dependencies, and the like, and she explains to her audience what these properties could imply for further data analysis, understanding, and interpretation.
	4.2 Know—understand—be able to interpret statistics commonly used with educational data (e.g., randomness, central tendencies, mean, standard deviation, significance)	Shortly after the steering meeting presentation, Laura meets her tutoring team to discuss the results of her research and possible implications for increasing the course completion rate. Laura shows her presentation, and she explains the common statistics (such as means and standard deviation) used with educational data with the help of tables and graphs. Having conducted some correlation and regression analyses to model the relationships between possible early indicators and actual dropouts, Laura further explains the ideas of significance testing to her team of student teaching assistants.
	4.3 Know—understand—be able to interpret insights from data analysis (e.g., explanations of patterns, identification of hypotheses, connection of multiple observations, underlying trends)	Laura explains some further insights from data analysis and educational data mining to her team. She illustrates trends in course participation and emergent patterns that differentiate successful learners from dropout learners. She discusses some possible interpretations with her team.
	4.4 Be able to elicit potential implications/links of the data analysis insights to instruction	In the following step, Laura relates the results and insights to the existing online tutoring strategy and maps out possible implications of a redesign. She identifies some crucial points in the course where special actions to prevent dropouts could be necessary. Together with her team, she then discusses possible tutoring strategies based on those insights. These alternative strategies focus on keeping the learners actively involved and include a number of tutorial interventions to achieve this.

(continued)

Table 4.3 (continued)

Dimension	Statement	Use-case e-trainer in higher education context
5. Data application	5.1 Know—understand—be able to use data analysis results to make decisions to revise instruction	As a result of their team effort, Laura writes up a report on how to change the tutoring in the MOOC based on the educational data at hand. She identifies the areas to be improved to prevent dropouts and makes clear and concrete suggestions for revised tutorial interventions and a support strategy based on the findings from data analysis. In the outlook section of her report, she discusses the potential of individualized process feedback based on learner data for keeping learners involved. These adaptive interventions could be implemented if the data analysis was carried out in real time and automatically as it is obligatory in a full-fledged learning analytics setting.
	5.2 Be able to evaluate the data-driven revision of instruction	Together with some experienced researchers from the project team, Laura develops a strategy on how to evaluate the impact of the data-driven tutoring strategy. In addition to plain completion rates, they define a set of indicators and criteria for measuring developments (i.e. use of learning objects, time-on-task, level of activity), and they sketch a methodologically sound A/B-design (i.e., a comparison of two different design cases with different tutoring "conditions" for preventing dropouts) for a quasi-experimental evaluation setting.
6. Data ethics	6.1 Know—understand—be able to use the informed consent	A major goal of the data-driven instruction project is to establish legal and ethics procedures. Thus, the project team collaborates intensively with the university's legal department, and they heavily discuss the various legal topics involved. As a first result, the project team develops a legally compliant participant form for informed consent to be presented to and signed by each person taking part in the MOOC on educational technology.
	6.2 Know—understand—be able to protect individuals' data privacy, confidentiality, integrity, and security	In the course of the discussion on legal aspects, the project team develops institutional guidelines to protect the learners' data privacy, confidentiality, integrity, and security.
	6.3 Know—understand—be able to apply authorship, ownership, data access (governance), renegotiation, and data sharing	Likewise, legal concepts like authorship, ownership, data access and governance, renegotiation, and data sharing are discussed. Well equipped with this specific knowledge, Laura writes a quick legal analysis for her data-driven online tutoring strategy.

4.3.2 Use-Case Example for e-Trainer in Higher Education Context

4.3.2.1 Background Story for e-Trainer Use-Case

Laura works as a full-time teaching assistant in the School of Education of an international university. One of her responsibilities is to coordinate the online support for the massive open online course "Introduction to Educational Technology." The course is offered on a major international MOOC platform, and it serves both as a marketing tool for the school and as an entry point to the school's certificate and degree programs in educational technology. Enrolment numbers were consistently high over recent semesters. However, dropout rates were notable as well, leaving ample space for improvement. Professor Chang, the course leader and main instructor, has decided to redesign the course and to implement some recent pedagogical innovations with the goal of increasing the course completion rate. Hence, data-driven instruction and learning analytics will be an important future topic area, and the course will be rebuilt on these approaches at the same time. Professor Chang sets up a project team with people involved in course design and implementation. Laura's task is to develop a tutoring and student support strategy that incorporates a data-driven approach to increase course completion. She is also responsible for implementing this strategy with her online tutoring team of three student teaching assistants.

4.3.2.2 Use-Case Activities for e-Trainer in Higher Education Context

Table 4.3 shows the L2A-EDL-CP use-case example for the e-trainer in higher education context linked to the dimensions/statements of the L2A-EDL-CP framework.

A short version of the use-case example for the e-trainer in higher education context is represented in Fig. 4.2.

4.3.3 Use-Case Example for the School Teacher of Blended Learning Courses in the K-12 Education Context

4.3.3.1 Background Story for the School Teacher Use-Case

Alice is an enthusiastic English language teacher who has just been appointed to an experimental high school in Athens, Greece. She will be responsible for the English language course of class 1 and class 2 of the ninth grade (14- to 15-year-old students). Alice is very excited about her new role. Nevertheless, the school's principal, Alex, is concerned about the relatively low performance of last year's eighth graders compared to other experimental schools in the region. Alex encourages Alice to use

Fig. 4.2 Use-case examples for for e-Trainer in Higher Education context

student data to gain insights and plan her teaching activities accordingly, so as to improve this year's Grade 9 students' academic performance. The principal also informs Alice about the learning management system (Moodle) used by the school to facilitate teaching and learning, pointing out that the previous teacher has already created some online activities there.

Alice decides to apply the flipped classroom strategy to her new students using the school's LMS. For this purpose, she designs and develops online teaching resources for class 1 and class 2. Students of these classes enrol in the respective group and study the lecture material at home (prior to the classroom meeting). The material is in the form of video, text, small activities with automatic feedback (such as online quizzes), and forum discussions. During the classroom sessions, students are performing more complex activities, typically in small groups, with the benefit of Alice's scaffolding, guidance, and feedback. Then, they can undertake some additional homework online to further check their understanding and extend their learning through appropriately designed individual and group assignments. Alice is confident with the flipped classroom approach, as she has used it before with great results. However, she is lacking data literacy competences. The principal encourages her to enrol in the Learn2Analyse MOOC before the school year starts—it is only an 8-week course, and it is free.

4.3.3.2   Use-Case Activities for the School Teacher in K-12 (Primary and Secondary) Blended Teaching and Learning Courses

Table 4.4 shows the L2A-EDL-CP use-case example for the school teacher in K-12 (primary and secondary) education context linked to the dimensions/statements of the L2A-EDL-CP framework.

A short version of the use-case example for the school teacher in K-12 (primary and secondary) is represented in Fig. 4.3.

Table 4.4 Use-case examples for the school teacher in K-12 blended courses linked to the L2A EDL-CP

Use-case school teacher in K-12 blended courses	Statement	Dimension
Alice starts posing questions to identify and **collect** the appropriate educational data. She asks herself, *"why do I need the data?" "what data are needed?" "where are data located?" "how will the data be collected?"* Alice decides to gather a variety of students' data, including demographics, perception data, past academic performance, last year's academic performance, and summative assessments for English language course and other relevant courses, as well as the regional performance data over the past 5 years. To retrieve the needed data, she has to access diverse sources: The school's internal data sources like the student information system as well as external data sources, like the district's databases.	1.1 Know—understand—be able to obtain, access, and gather the appropriate data and/or data sources	1. Data collection
To this end, she contacts her colleague, appointed as the school's data protection officer (DPO), to secure all necessary approvals for the sources handled by her school or by the corresponding district. As soon as Alice signs the required data protection consent form, she gets permission to download the data sets from the several sources. Alice also requests to be granted access to the LMS used by the school (a new teacher account is created by the LMS administrator). Before implementing her flipped classroom strategy, she contacts the school's DPO again to discuss any legal and ethical issues she needs to pay attention to. As advised by the DPO, she accesses the LMS, and via the *"user agreements"* page, she reviews the existing user agreements and confirms that *signed informed consent* has been given for all participating students (either parental consent on behalf of minors or directly by the students, as defined by the *National Data Protection Authority*). Alice imports all retrieved data sets into her spreadsheet software to further process them.	6.1 Know—understand—be able to use the informed consent	6. Data ethics

(continued)

Table 4.4 (continued)

Use-case school teacher in K-12 blended courses	Statement	Dimension
Alice gets informed by the DPO on school's policy and guidelines to protect students' *data privacy, confidentiality, integrity,* and *security*. She becomes aware of the appropriate technical and organizational measures taken by the school, so as to secure data protection. Such measures include the use of anonymization and pseudonymization to remove personally identifiable information, encryption, limited accessibility, as well as a short storage period. Alice needs to pay extra attention to *sensitive* data, a special category of personal data, e.g., ethnic origin and health-related data, since the school can only process this data under specific conditions. Alice also gets informed about the school's *LMS GDPR compliance* functionality, which is designed to assist in ensuring that the online course is fully compliant with the General Data Protection regulation (GDPR) requirements. Some key features include an age check for the new LMS users, management of the user agreements to privacy policies, data export and deletion requests, definition and maintenance of a data registry, as well as the ability to give consent on behalf of minors.	6.2 Know—understand—be able to protect individuals' data privacy, confidentiality, integrity, and security	6. Data ethics
Alice gets familiar with key legal concepts including authorship, *ownership, data access* and *governance, renegotiation,* and *data sharing*. Alice realizes that though the presumption is often that data collected is owned by the school, nevertheless, the school does not own the student data that it holds, but has temporary stewardship according to GDPR. Alice is now ready to cope with any ethical issue that may arise, and she is confident that she can proceed further with her flipped classroom strategy, making it a success story for her students.	6.3 Know—understand—be able to apply authorship, ownership, data access (governance), renegotiation, and data sharing	6. Data ethics

(continued)

Table 4.4 (continued)

Use-case school teacher in K-12 blended courses	Statement	Dimension
After running the online course for 3 weeks, Alice checks the data about students' activities which have been tracked by the online learning environment so far. Thus, she also *collects* data related to students' engagement, behavior, and performance within the LMS, e.g., time spent in the platform, the videos her students watched, their progress in the online elements of the course, the downloaded files, their online quiz scores, their participation in the forum, as well as interaction between peers.	1.1 Know—understand—be able to obtain, access and gather the appropriate data and/or data sources	1. Data collection
Before proceeding further, Alice confirms that the collected data meets basic quality characteristics. Thus, she examines and verifies the educational data against different *quality measures,* such as *relevancy* (the data must directly relate to the questions she posed), *reliability* (the data must be measured, trustworthy, and consistent), and *validity* (the data must measure what she intends to measure). Alice pays attention to avoid biases, e.g., *availability bias,* by collecting the data that are easier to obtain, rather than collecting more relevant data.	1.2 Know—understand—be able to apply data limitations and quality measures (e.g., validity, reliability, biases in the data, difficulty in collection, accuracy, completeness)	1. Data collection

(continued)

Table 4.4 (continued)

Use-case school teacher in K-12 blended courses	Statement	Dimension

Alice studies the performance of her students based on data collected so far.
She wants to create a table that merges data from both sources: The school's central students' information system as well as the LMS. Alice soon realizes that since the data comes from various sources in diverse formats, the results are quite messy, containing missing values, outliers, and duplicate instances. To obtain a consistent database, free from any sort of discrepancies, *data cleaning* is required so as to detect erroneous or irrelevant data and discard it.
She notices that many problems arise:
  Inconsistent formats for input fields, such as the mixed use of American (MM/DD/YYYY) and European (DD/MM/YYYY) date format.
  To be able to correctly merge the data from the two sources, it is necessary to use a unique identifier for each student that exists in both tables (e.g., registration number).
  There are students who changed schools and do not appear in this year's data.
  There is no direct connection between the groups because a number of students changed classes from last year.
Thus, Alice applies data cleaning and *organizing* so as to get a concrete data set. For this task, Alice is supported by the school's technical team in using open source tools for data cleaning, like *OpenRefine*.[a]
	2.1 Know—understand—be able to apply data processing and handling methods (i.e., methods for cleaning and changing data to make it more organized—e.g., duplication, data structuring)	2. Data management

In order to better describe and characterize the produced structured data set, Alice decides to look for the appropriate *metadata* schema to ensure that each data element is defined the same way throughout the school's organization. Following this schema, Alice, with the support of her school's technical team, applies *descriptive metadata* (such as subject, grade level, timestamp, and related skills), *administrative metadata* (such as rights and licensing), and *structural metadata* (such as parts, prerequisites) to describe the respective data elements.	2.2 Know—understand—be able to apply data description (i.e., metadata)	2. Data management

(continued)

Table 4.4 (continued)

Use-case school teacher in K-12 blended courses	Statement	Dimension
It's now the time for Alice to apply the needed *curation* processes to the integrated data, always with the support of her school's technical team. Through the curation process, the resulting composite data set is well organized, enhanced, and reliably retrievable for future reuse. The goal is to maintain the value of the unified data set and ensure its long-term availability. To this end, Alice determines what data is worth saving and for how long, especially considering the high volume of the resulting data set. She addresses the DPO to define a data *preservation plan* according to which the performance data are transferred every semester to the corresponding school database for permanent storage, while the tracking data remains at the LMS until students' graduation.	2.3 Know—understand—be able to apply data curation processes (i.e., to ensure that data is reliably retrievable for future reuse and to determine what data is worth saving and for how long)	2. Data management
Having prepared the data, Alice needs to ensure its *preservation*. Alice gets informed about the hybrid storage solution used by the school. It's a combination of local infrastructure/data center and cloud-based storage. Moreover, as per her school guidelines for data storage good practice strategy, she needs to create multiple independent copies to stabilize her files. The copies are geographically separated in different locations, using different storage technologies, and are actively monitored to ensure any problems are detected and corrected.	2.4 Know—understand—be able to apply the technologies to preserve data (i.e., store, persist, maintain, backup data), e.g., storage mediums/ services, tools, mechanisms	2. Data management
Now that the data is ready to yield powerful insights, Alice proceeds with analysis and modeling methods. Initially, she applies *descriptive statistics* for the last year's class 1 and class 2 eighth graders. Alice calculates the *total mean, median,* and *standard deviation* of her students' last year's final scores, so as to get a measure of their general performance. She is also interested in learning whether there is a correlation between time spent in the LMS and student's performance on quizzes (*inferential statistics*).	3.1 Know—understand—be able to apply data analysis and modeling methods (e.g., application of descriptive statistics, exploratory data analysis, data mining)	3. Data analysis

(continued)

Table 4.4 (continued)

Use-case school teacher in K-12 blended courses	Statement	Dimension
To gain a better understanding of the data on hand, Alice proceeds with its *pictorial visualization*. This will also assist her in preparing for the upcoming meeting with the school's principal in order to present her findings. Firstly, Alice decides to graphically present the last year's overall students' academic performance. Thus, she plots a *histogram* to visualize the underlying *frequency distribution*. This helps her ascertain the number of students who are performing to a particular standard. To further enhance her understanding of spread, Alice also utilizes a *boxplot*, which includes minimum, maximum, median, first, and third quartile. Based on the gathered LMS access data, Alice also produces a *scatter plot* that shows the relationship between students' activity time in the LMS and their performance on quizzes.	3.2 Know—understand—be able to apply data presentation methods (e.g., pictorial visualization of the data by using graphs, charts, maps, and other data forms like textual or tabular representations)	3. Data analysis
Following data analysis, Alice is keen to comprehend the story that the collected data reveals. She starts by interpreting *data properties*, including measurement errors, outliers, discrepancies, and data dependencies. For last year's academic performance, Alice notices that the total class mean may be more or less significant depending on the number and extent of outliers in the distribution of grades. She *appreciates the impact of extreme scores on the mean.*	4.1 Know—understand—be able to interpret data properties (e.g., measurement error, outliers, discrepancies within data, key takeaway points, data dependencies)	4. Data comprehension and interpretation

(continued)

Table 4.4 (continued)

Use-case school teacher in K-12 blended courses	Statement	Dimension
Alice realizes that she can't rely on the total class *mean* value. The *median* may be more helpful than the mean depending on outliers. With regard to *standard deviation*, the larger the standard deviation, the larger the spread of student performance within the class. With regard to the scatter plot, at first glance, it does not suggest a strong relationship between course activity time and quizzes' performance. Most students do not seem to fit into the "ideal" or "predictable" model: If students spend time and study hard, they will perform well. Following a closer look, it seems that it also reveals four "unique" data points: Two students Ann and David appeared to be quite active in the course (49 and 60 hours, respectively), but did not do as well as the rest of the students did. One student, John, was not so active (20 hours) but did reasonably well, whereas Peter spent the least amount of time (about 2 hours) in the course compared to the rest of the class. However he excelled on quiz assignments. Alice understands that further analysis is needed. She needs to drill into the LMS activities for these students.	4.2 Know—understand—be able to interpret statistics commonly used with educational data (e.g., randomness, central tendencies, mean, standard deviation, significance)	4. Data comprehension and interpretation

(continued)

Table 4.4 (continued)

Use-case school teacher in K-12 blended courses	Statement	Dimension
Alice learns that her school's LMS (Moodle) provides a number of useful learning analytics tools. She decides to leverage them and implement more complex analyses and statistical models. To this end, Alice implements *descriptive learning analytics* by using the "*learning analytics enriched rubric*[b]" tool, an advanced grading method used for criteria-based assessment. Grading levels are associated to data from the analysis of learners' interaction and learning behavior within the online elements of her course, such as the number of post messages, times of accessing learning material, assignments' grades, and so on. She also decides to use "*inspire analytics*,[c]" a tool for *predictive learning analytics*, which provides feedback about a student's progress against a range of indicators and activities identified to have an impact on student success in the online course. In order for Alice to examine further the quizzes' results, she generates a respective "*quiz statistics report*[d]" for each one including details of the attempts of the enrolled students (how long the student's attempt took, the student's grade for each individual question). She focuses on two of her students, Ann and David, who do not perform well. For these two students, she also retrieves a "*complete report*[e]" that displays a very detailed view of the progress of the individual learner throughout the online elements of her course (a list of the course activities and resources and how often and when the user has accessed them). Using this report, Alice can obtain more accurate information on students' progress and engagement. She confirms that Ann and David struggle with content comprehension.	4.3 Know—understand—be able to interpret insights from data analysis (e.g., explanations of patterns, identification of hypotheses, connection of multiple observations, underlying trends)	4. Data comprehension and interpretation

(continued)

Table 4.4 (continued)

Use-case school teacher in K-12 blended courses	Statement	Dimension
Using learning analytics, Alice is self-reflecting to improve the design and delivery of her course. She uses learning analytics to monitor their learning process, to discover patterns, to identify problems early, to find indicators for success and indicators for poor marks or dropout. Using prescriptive learning analytics, Alice applies the "*analytics and recommendations*[6]" tool, so as to get a visual color-coded presentation of the student's participation in each online course activity, as well as some initial recommendations about what activities students could work on to improve their final grade. She realizes that some students, like John, do not participate in the forums at all. This behavior reflects his low interaction in class activities, as well. And then, there is Peter whose performance is remarkable though he does not seem interested in the online activities, as he goes right from the homepage of the online course to assignments/quizzes without additional navigation.	4.4 Be able to elicit potential implications/ links of the data analysis insights to instruction	4. Data comprehension and interpretation

(continued)

Table 4.4 (continued)

Use-case school teacher in K-12 blended courses	Statement	Dimension
Based on the results of her data analysis, Alice decides to revise the course's online learning activities and educational resources. Thus, she uses the course level *"activity report[g]"* to investigate how her students engaged with the different elements of the course and which activities were the most appealing. The activity report provides aggregate reports highlighting which elements of the course have more or less student activity. To support students who are struggling, like Ann and David, Alice decides to include *"lesson activities[h]"* to incorporate conditional branching and create differentiated learning paths by sequencing learning activities throughout a series of web pages. In the event that a student answers a question incorrectly, conditional branching makes it possible to direct the student to additional content pages to help them reach the correct answer. Each question response could "jump" the student to various areas of content within the same lesson activity. Moreover, she includes additional *graded discussion forums* to facilitate a higher participation and support further the students when they study on their own, allowing them to ask questions and receive support. To drive motivation for students like Peter, she also assigns optional challenging activities. To further increase students' engagement and participation, she also decides to add *level up!—Gamification,[i]* an easy way to gamify students' learning experience by motivating them to progress towards the next level of the course.	5.1 Know—understand—be able to use data analysis results to make decisions to revise instruction	5. Data application
Furthermore, Alice designs an evaluation plan for her course. She plans to use indicators to ensure that the flipped classroom initiative is on track for reaching the long-term goal of improving students' academic performance to reach the regional standards. Her data literacy awareness and competences, including the use of available tools, have helped her collect useful evidence (based on data analysis) for herself, her principal, and the parents.	5.2 Be able to evaluate the data-driven revision of instruction	5. Data application

[a]https://openrefine.org/
[b]https://docs.moodle.org/311/en/Learning_Analytics_Enriched_Rubric

(continued)

Table 4.4 (continued)

[c]https://moodle.org/plugins/tool_inspire
[d]https://docs.moodle.org/310/en/Quiz_statistics_report
[e]https://docs.moodle.org/310/en/Activity_report
[f]https://moodle.org/plugins/block_analytics_recommendations
[g]https://docs.moodle.org/310/en/Activity_report
[h]https://docs.moodle.org/311/en/Lesson_activity
[i]https://moodle.org/plugins/block_xp

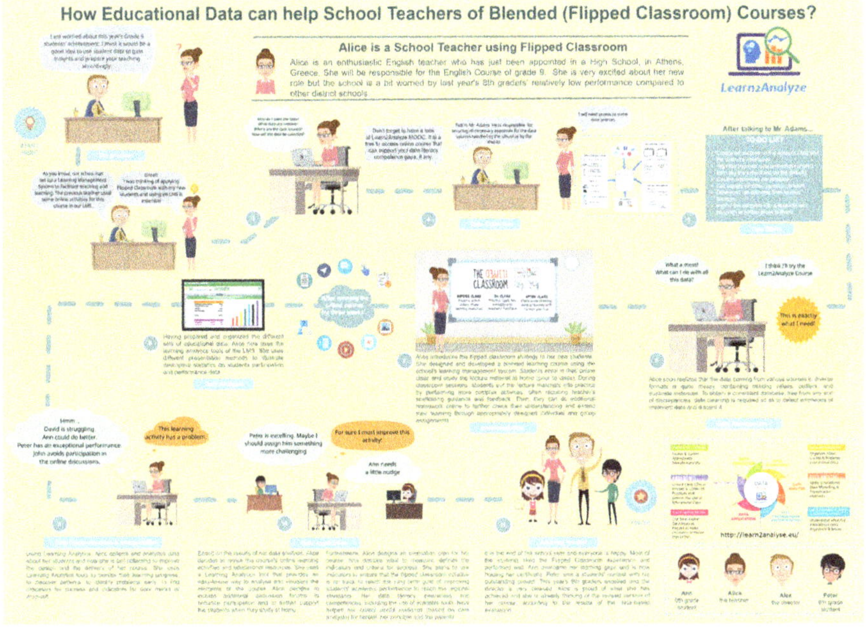

Fig. 4.3 Use-case examples for the school teacher of blended learning courses in the K-12 education context

Chapter 5
Conclusions and Future Direction

Abstract This chapter discusses conclusions and suggestions for future plans based on the lessons learnt through the development and validation of the Learn2Analyze Educational Data Literacy Competence Profile (L2A-EDL-CP). Given the lessons learnt during the L2A project life and taking into consideration the new opportunities and challenges that emerged during the Covid-19 pandemic lockdown, the consortium partners have recognized the need for a European Educational Data Literacy Academy for Educators that will integrate and extend the knowledge and results of the L2A project. Such an initiative will need to include academic and research partners, e-learning industry partners, as well as vocational education and training (VET) providers. Such an initiative will be offering professional development courses and micro-credential certifications on various educational data literacy competences at different levels.

Keywords Educational data literacy · Educational data analytics · Teaching and learning analytics · Online and blended learning · Competence profiles · Teacher education and professional development

Given the lessons learnt during the L2A project life and taking into consideration the new opportunities and challenges that emerged during the Covid-19 pandemic lockdown, the consortium partners have recognized the need for a *European Educational Data Literacy Academy for Educators* that will integrate and extend the knowledge and results of the L2A project. Such an initiative will need to include academic and research partners, e-learning industry partners, as well as vocational education and training (VET) providers. Such an initiative will be offering professional development courses and micro-credential certifications on various educational data literacy competences at different levels. The rationale behind this future direction is twofold.

On the one hand, the "upskilling imperative" of educational data literacy has been identified as fundamental for the digital readiness of educational organizations and professionals, including K-12 school teachers and leaders, to stay attuned to the new technological advances and the fast-changing labor market demands and to

D. Sampson et al., *Educational Data Literacy*, Advances in Analytics for Learning and Teaching, https://doi.org/10.1007/978-3-031-11705-3_5

deal effectively with the modern social and economic challenges. This immediate need is even more emphasized considering (i) the wake of the unprecedented crisis of the Covid-19 global pandemic that brought to the forefront the urgent demand for technology-supported remote teaching, calling on education systems to take immediate actions to support creative, flexible, and inclusive education and training in the long term; (ii) online learning environments and the use of educational data in teaching, learning, and assessment raise challenges such as ethical issues and implications, especially in terms of privacy, security of data, and informed consent that should be addressed via transparent and well-defined ethical policies and codes of practices.

Surprisingly, although data-driver decision-making in education is very high on the agenda of national, European, and international education policies (mainly for external accountability purposes and data-based evidence collection but also for taking more informed decisions for day-to-day teaching and learning), there are very limited opportunities for either professional development or university courses on educational data literacy. The SHEILA project, supported by the Erasmus+ Programme of the European Union [562080-EPP-1-2015-1-BE-EPPKA3-PI-FORWARD], has recognized in their concluding public report (Nov 2018) that there is a skills gap in educational data analytics and that "it is crucial to equip key users with reflective skills to interpret data and turn it into constructive action" (Tsai et al., 2018).

The Learn2Analyze project has developed and validated a competence profile for e-learning professionals and educators and has also designed, developed, and extensively evaluated a competence-based MOOC for explicitly cultivating this competence profile. The results of the pilot implementation of the Learn2Analyze MOOC showed that the majority of the participants were K-12 teachers and HE students (approximately 62%). Therefore, the consortium can build on the lessons learnt and the results of the L2A project, to address the needs of the largest professional group in the education sector, namely, K-12 organizations and educators (school leaders, teachers, and pre-service higher education students) for certified educational data literacy professional competences.

To this end, the consortium can embrace the research, development, and validation of the comprehensive competence profile for educational data literacy in order to inform existing competence profiles for educators, such as the European Framework for the Digital Competence of Educators—DigCompEdu (Redecker, 2017), educational leaders, and educational organizations, such as the European Framework for Digitally-Competent Educational Organizations—DigiCompOrg (Kampylis et al., 2015).

More specifically, the European Framework for the Digital Competence of Educators (DigCompEdu) includes the digital competences of analyzing evidence and feedback and planning, which are closely related to the use of educational data analytics, among the required competences so that educators "are to be able to seize the potential of digital technologies for enhancing and innovating education."

Thus, the consortium partners plan to capitalize on and extend the Learn2Analyze EDL-CP for educational organizations and educators (including in-service school teachers and school leaders and pre-service higher education students) by focusing on the European reference framework's DigCompEdu Progression Model (through the development of suitable grid/rubric for each competence and respective statements of the EDL-CP framework describing in detail the expected learning outcomes in terms of knowledge and skills, across different proficiency levels based on the complexity of tasks and autonomy, and providing examples that could be applied by HE students, teachers, and school leaders to their professional field). The guidelines of these extended competence frameworks can be accompanied by a self-assessment tool for educators and educational organizations to steer the self-reflection process for evaluating their strengths and weaknesses in their educational data readiness. Furthermore, in order to accredit these new competences, innovative online professional competence-based certification programs are also required, adequately designed to meet the needs of EDL, where micro-credentials can play a key role in more flexible and inclusive learning paths, enabling broader professional development opportunities and strengthening the role of higher education and vocational education and training institutions in lifelong learning.

Appendices

Appendix A: The Generic Competence Dimensions and Competence Statements of Existing Educational Data Literacy Competence Frameworks

EF1: Data Science Competence Framework (CF-DS) (Demchenko & Belloum, 2017)

Table A.1 Data-related competence statements of the EF1

EF1 Demchenko and Belloum (2017)
Competence statements
5
Develop and implement a data management strategy for data collection, storage, preservation, and availability for further processing
Develop and manage/supervise policies on data protection, privacy, IPR, and ethical issues in data management
Implement data protection, backup, privacy, mechanisms/services, comply with IPR, ethics, and responsible data use
Ethics and responsible use of data and insight delivered, awareness of dependability (data scientist is a feedback loop in data-driven companies)
Adhere to high ethical and professional norms, responsible use of power data-driven technologies, avoid and disregard unethical use of technologies and biased data collection and presentation

D. Sampson et al., *Educational Data Literacy*, Advances in Analytics for Learning and Teaching, https://doi.org/10.1007/978-3-031-11705-3

EF2: Ten Simple Rules for Responsible Big Data Research (Zook et al., 2017)

Table A.2 Data-related competence statements of the EF2

EF2-Zook et al. (2017)
Competence statements
10
Acknowledge that data are people and can do harm
Recognize that privacy is more than a binary value
Guard against the reidentification of your data
Practice ethical data sharing
Consider the strengths and limitations of your data; big does not automatically mean better
Debate the tough, ethical choices
Develop a code of conduct for your organization, research community, or industry
Design your data and systems for auditability
Engage with the broader consequences of data and analysis practices
Know when to break these rules

EF3: Guidelines for the Ethical Use of Digital Data in Human Research (Clark et al., 2015)

Table A.3 Data-related competence statements of the EF3

EF3-Clark et al. (2015)
Competence statements
12
Consent (*gaining informed consent to collect personal data and material posted on social media, including social networking sites, audio-, photo-, and video-sharing sites, blogs and microblogs, wikis, chat rooms, and virtual worlds as sources of research data*)—data can only be used if they are de-identified, that is, anonymized.
Notice and transparency (*individuals must be made aware of when personal information about them is collected, by whom, and for what purpose*).
Re-negotiate consent if data are to be used by someone other than the person who collected it or is to be repurposed in another context than the one it was collected in use of digital data only with explicit permission.
Authentication of subjects (*issues of consent, duty of care, and harm in relation to participants may be compounded by a lack of knowledge about who participants really are (digital identities)*).
Consent and use limitation (*an individual's consent is required in order to collect personal information about them; personal information can only be collected for specified purposes, and the subsequent use of that information is limited to those purposes*).
Protecting privacy and confidentiality (*define mechanisms, regulatory frameworks, or administrative structures to protect the individual's privacy and confidentiality in relation to the project*).
Access and participation (*individuals have the right to access personal data that refers to them. In case that stored data contains any inaccuracies, individuals may also require that errors be corrected*).

(continued)

Table A.3 (continued)

EF3-Clark et al. (2015)
Competence statements
12
Integrity and security (*collectors of personal information must make reasonable efforts to ensure data is accurate and up-to-date; also protect against unauthorized access, disclosure, or use*).
Enforcement and accountability (*the collectors of personal information must be accountable for any failures to comply with the previous principles*).
Authorship and ownership of digital data (*clarify information ownership, who is in control of access, who is charged with managing the data, who may be considered responsible for the data, who has long-term responsibility for the quality of the data, the protection of sensitive material and the long-term maintenance of the data*).
Data governance and custodianship (*clarify who is responsible for storage, management, and access to data; establish good data governance practices in order to ensure data security and thus protect participants' privacy and confidentiality*).
Data-sharing (*clarify where data reuse must be approved or justified under the same framework as the original use of the data—Reduce unnecessary duplication and competition*).

EF4: Data Ethics Framework (Hancock, 2018)

Table A.4 Data-related competence statements of the EF4

EF4-Hancock (2018)
Competence statements
7
Start with a clear user's need and public benefit (*description of the user's need with supporting evidence*)
Be aware of relevant legislation and codes of practice (*list the pieces of legislation, codes of practice, and guidance that apply to your project*)
Use data that is proportionate to the user's needs (*describe how the data being used is proportional to the user's need*)
Understand the limitations of the data (*identify the potential limitations of the data source(s) and how they are being mitigated*)
Use robust practices and work within your skillset (*explain the relevant expertise and approaches that are being employed to maximize the efficacy of the project*)
Make your work transparent and be accountable (*describe how you have considered making your work transparent and accountable*)
Embed data use responsibly (*describe the steps taken to ensure any new model, policy, or service is managed responsibly*)

EF5: A Unified Ethical Frame for Big Data Analysis—Big Data Ethics Initiative (IAF, 2015)

Table A.5 Data-related competence statements of the EF5

EF5-IAF (2015)
Competence statements
5
Ethical data use should be done with an expectation of tangible benefit—define the usefulness or merit that comes from solving the problem
If the anticipated improvements can be achieved in a less data-intensive manner, then less intensive processing should be pursued
Big data insights, when placed into production, should provide value that is sustainable over a reasonable time frame (data sustainability, algorithmic sustainability, device, and/or manufacturer-based sustainability)
Respect the individuals to whom the data pertains, organizations that originate the data, organizations that aggregate the data and those that might regulate the data
Conduct analysis of fairness needs to look not only at protecting against unseemly or risky actions but also at enhancing beneficial opportunities

EF6: The Data Ethics Canvas (ODI, 2017)

Table A.6 Data-related competence statements of the EF6

EF6-ODI (2017)
Competence statements
15
Name and describe key data sources used in your project, whether you're collecting them yourself or getting access from third parties
Identify limitations in your data sources (e.g., biases, sensitivity)
If sharing data with other organizations, define with whom and under which conditions
Consider data protection legislation, IP and database rights legislation, anti-discrimination laws, sector- specific data sharing policies/regulations (e.g., health, employment, taxation), sector-specific ethics legislation
Determine the rights to data sources
Cite existing ethical frameworks that are relevant to your project
Justify your reason for using this data (primary purpose, benefits)
Communicate your purpose of using data with the people from whom the data come
Explain what the positive effects are on people
Explain what are the negative effects are on people
Explain actions taken to minimize the negative impact
Engaging with people (*how and to what degree they can appeal or request changes to the service*)
Communicate potential risks and issues to the people who the data come from
Reviews and iterations (*explain how ongoing issues related to data ethics will be monitored and discussed*)
Determine the actions taken

Appendix B: Educational Data Literacy Professional Development and University Courses

Appendix B.1—Courses' Overview

Title of the course	[1] Data Literacy 01 (http://artofeducating.com/online-courses/)
Type of course	Professional development
Targeted audience	Practicing school administrators and teachers from kindergarten to high school in any subject area
Offered by	Art of educating (Jennifer L. Morrison)
Means of delivery	Blended
Cost	Fees are applied
Duration	15 weeks
Expected workload to study the course	At minimum three or more hours per week listening, participating, and completing the course activities.
Learning objectives	Define reliability and validity in classroom terms Define data literacy and explain why educators need to be data literate Give good reasons why educators don't necessarily jump up and down with excitement about data and assessment Know what you can do to own and spread the data literacy story in your context Recognize that data are more than standardized test scores Gather four types of data in your own context Reinforce and support your learning and data literacy development Define classroom research and how it might improve learning in your classroom and/or school Generate and share potential research questions Identify appropriate data sources for conducting your research
Link with existing EDL competence framework	–
Structure	Unit 1—Understanding the role of data Unit 2—Creating reliable classroom assessments Unit 3—Harnessing classroom research to improve student learning Course wrap-up
Method of assessment	Assignments (at the end of each lesson, students will be asked to complete an activity and share it with other members of their class through lesson-specific discussion forums).
Comment why this is a useful course to include in the review	This course will ground learners in her eight principles of data literacy, with the goal of empowering them to collect and use them more effectively.

(continued)

Title of the course	[2] Analytics for the Classroom Teacher (https://www.edx.org/course/analytics- for-the-classroom-teacher)
Type of course	University course
Targeted audience	Teachers, instructional designers
Offered by	Curtin University via edX
Means of delivery	MOOC
Cost	Free (open)—Verified certificate (paid)
Duration	6 weeks
Expected workload to study the course	3–4 hours per week
Learning objectives	How educational data analytics can improve classroom teaching and learning, as well as supporting data—Driven decision making at various levels of school operations An understanding of the current state-of-the-art in teaching and learning analytics tools and methods How teaching analytics can be used to analyse your lesson plans How learning analytics can be used to analyse the classroom delivery of your lesson plan and reveal more about your students' learning How you can reflect on your teaching practice by combining insights from both teaching and learning analytics
Link with existing EDL competence framework	–
Structure	Module 1—Introduction to educational data for supporting data-driven decision making in school education Module 2—Teaching analytics: Analyze your lesson plans to improve them Module 3—Learning analytics: Analyze the classroom delivery of your lesson plans and discover more about your students Module 4—Teaching and learning analytics to support teacher inquiry Module 5—Conclusion
Method of assessment	Online quiz
Comment why this is a useful course to include in the review	This course will teach learners how teachers, curriculum developers, and policy makers are collecting and analyzing data from the classroom to help guide decisions at all levels. Learners will get a deeper understanding of how data analytics can help them to make improvements in students' learning.

Title of the course	[3] Learning Analytics Fundamentals (https://www.edx.org/course/learning- analytics-fundamentals-utarlingtonx-link-la-fundx)
Type of course	University course
Targeted audience	Those who have a bachelor's degree and are interested in developing learning and data science skills for employment in education, corporate, non-profit, and military sectors.
Offered by	University of Texas at Arlington via edX
Means of delivery	MOOC
Cost	Free (open)—verified certificate (paid)

Title of the course	[3] Learning Analytics Fundamentals (https://www.edx.org/course/ learning- analytics-fundamentals-utarlingtonx-link-la-fundx)
Duration	4 weeks
Expected workload to study the course	5–7 hours per week
Learning objectives	The field of learning analytics and explore how data and information are used Common learning analytics methods and approaches, such as data wrangling and cleaning, structure discovery, and basic prediction modelling How to conduct basic data wrangling and analyses Ethics and privacy considerations Working in a collaborative, cross-disciplinary setting Common toolsets used in the UTArlingtonX learning analytics courses (R in RStudio and Jupiter notebooks)
Link with existing EDL competence framework	–
Structure	Instructor lecture videos Guest lecture and interview videos Supplemental reading Discussion forums Working with learning data in R, R studio, swirl, and Jupyter notebooks Ethics scenario assignment
Method of assessment	Assignments in R (30% of total grade) Ethics scenario (20% of total grade) Participation (50% of total grade)
Comment why this is a useful course to include in the review	After completing this course, learners will have a better understanding of the field of learning analytics and be able to apply skills to any occupation that utilizes educational data.

Title of the course	[4] Big Data and Education (https://www.edx.org/course/ big-data-education-pennx-bde1x-0)
Type of course	University course
Targeted audience	Teachers, instructional designers
Offered by	University of Pennsylvania via edX
Means of delivery	MOOC
Cost	Free (open)—verified certificate (paid)
Duration	8 weeks
Expected workload to study the course	6–12 hours per week
Learning objectives	Key methods for educational data mining How to apply methods using standard tools such as RapidMiner How to use methods to answer practical educational questions
Link with existing EDL competence framework	–

(continued)

Title of the course	[4] Big Data and Education (https://www.edx.org/course/big-data-education-pennx-bde1x-0)
Structure	Week 1: Prediction Week 2: Diagnostic metrics and cross-validation Week 3: Feature engineering and behavior detection Week 4: Knowledge inference and knowledge structures Week 5: Relationship mining Week 6: Visualization Week 7: Structure discovery Week 8: Discovery with models Wrapping up
Method of assessment	Assignments
Comment why this is a useful course to include in the review	Methods for mining and modeling the increasing amounts of fine-grained data about learners are being developed; in this class, learners will learn about these methods, and their strengths and weaknesses for different applications. Thus they will be able to use each method to answer education research questions and to drive intervention and improvement in educational software and systems.

Title of the course	[5] Data, Analytics and Learning (https://www.edx.org/course/data-analytics-learning-utarlingtonx-link5-10x)
Type of course	University course
Targeted audience	Teachers, instructional designers
Offered by	University of Texas at Arlington via edX
Means of delivery	MOOC
Cost	Free (open)
Duration	9 weeks
Expected workload to study the course	5 hours/week
Learning objectives	How to identify trade-offs between proprietary and open source tools commonly used in learning analytics The learning analytics data cycle How to perform social network analysis, interpret the analysis for the study of networked learning, and visualize the analysis results in Gephi Training and evaluating classifiers that use clickstream data, with a focus on how to engineer features and training labels Evaluation issues, key diagnostic metrics and their uses, and validity issues How to approach a problem in the area of text mining using LightSIDE, how to engineer features for text classification, how to use LightSIDE for automated collaborative learning process analysis How trained models can be used in service of learning research
Link with existing EDL competence framework	–

(continued)

Title of the course	[5] Data, Analytics and Learning (https://www.edx.org/course/ data-analytics-learning-utarlingtonx-link5-10x)
Structure	*Week 1*: Introduction to learning analytics (LA) *Week 2*: Starting with data *Week 3*: Basics of social network analysis *Week 4*: Sensemaking of social network analysis for learning *Week 5*: Prediction modeling *Week 6*: Behavior detection and model assessment *Week 7*: Text mining introduction *Week 8*: Text mining nuts and bolts *Week 9*: Wrapping up
Method of assessment	Weekly assignments
Comment why this is a useful course to include in the review	This course is a great introduction to the logic and methods of analysis of data to improve teaching and learning

Title of the course	[6] Practical Learning Analytics (https://www.edx.org/course/ practical-learning- analytics-michiganx-plax)
Type of course	University course
Targeted audience	Post-secondary students, faculty, and staff, along with those outside the academy who are interested in understanding it—people in foundations, the educational technology industry, or the government.
Offered by	University of Michigan via edX
Means of delivery	MOOC
Cost	Free (open)
Duration	4 weeks
Expected workload to study the course	2–8 hours per week
Learning objectives	About the landscape of learning analytics in higher education How to bring in data of your own for analysis and visualization About performance prediction in a course: up to and including grade penalties, placement analyses, performance disparities and their correlates, course-to- course correlation How institutions are creating early warning systems and personalized communication How to apply learning analytics to observe differences and probe impact, capturing more and better information
Link with existing EDL competence framework	–
Structure	Setting the table Five courses—each with an overview, data, tools, and a creative extension competition Clearing up

(continued)

Title of the course	[6] Practical Learning Analytics (https://www.edx.org/course/ practical-learning- analytics-michiganx-plax)
Method of assessment	One group of users will be expected to participate only in the core material of each week, perhaps 4–8 hours total of watching, reading, and responding. Each week's core material will include short quizzes on core content, along with discussion prompts for use in the forums. A second group will go slightly deeper, visiting some of the five courses, selecting the small plates. The hungry diners: The third group will complete at least some of the full courses, adapting the code which is provided of developing their own R code to determine things about the data which the instructors' examples don't support.
Comment why this is a useful course to include in the review	After completing this course, learners should emerge with a deeper appreciation for what we might learn from the data they already have, with knowledge of either the general nature or the gory details of some specific applications, and with excitement about the possibilities afforded by the richer data which is coming soon.

Title of the course	[7] Data Literacy for School Teachers—EDPZ6012 (https://www. sydney.edu.au/courses/units-of-study/2022/edpz/edpz6012.html)
Type of course	University course (unit of study)
Targeted audience	Teachers, instructional designers
Offered by	University of Sydney
Means of delivery	Blended
Cost	Fee are applied
Duration	2 hours × 13 weeks
Expected workload to study the course	Not mentioned
Learning objectives	To understand and use data effectively To inform teaching and learning decisions
Link with existing EDL competence framework	–
Structure	List of topics in bullets
Method of assessment	Formative assessment and engagement 1000wds (20%) and a major project with 3 assignments 5500 wds (80%)
Comment why this is a useful course to include in the review	This course is completely focused on EDL.

Title of the course	[8] Advancing computational and data literacy skills schools for life scientists (http://www.nhm.ac.uk/our-science/courses-and-students/ advancing-computational-and-data-literacy-for-life-scientists.html)
Type of course	Professional development
Targeted audience	PhD students and early career researchers in the field of computational and data literacy teaching

Title of the course	[8] Advancing computational and data literacy skills schools for life scientists (http://www.nhm.ac.uk/our-science/courses-and-students/advancing-computational-and-data-literacy-for-life-scientists.html)
Offered by	Berkeley Institute for Data Science (Dr Karthik Ram) Natural History Museum (Dr Natalie Cooper) Denison University (Dr Sarah Supp)
Means of delivery	Blended
Cost	Fee are applied
Duration	5 days
Expected workload to study the course	–
Learning objectives	Train participants in data literacy skills Efficient collection of data and metadata for future analyses Data wrangling, tidying, and organization in R Data visualization and analysis in R Teach participants basic tools for reproducible science reproducible report creation version control Introduce participants to Open Science principles and procedures Data archiving options and best practice Code sharing options and best practice Introduce participants to the fundamentals of programming basics in R and The principles of tidy code and code review Create a community of data literate scientists
Link with existing EDL competence framework	–
Structure	Short lectures Computer practicals Putting skills into practice using data gathered in the Museum's "behind the scenes" collections Optional evening activities where participants can network with each other, and with members of London's data science community
Method of assessment	Not mentioned
Comment why this is a useful course to include in the review	This really practical and interactive course has been designed by professionals in the field of EDL.

Title of the course	[9] Introduction to Data Wise: A Collaborative Process to Improve Learning & Teaching (https://www.edx.org/course/introduction-to-data-wise-a-collaborative-process)
Type of course	University course
Targeted audience	Teachers, instructional designers
Offered by	Harvard University via edX
Means of delivery	Online

(continued)

Title of the course	[9] Introduction to Data Wise: A Collaborative Process to Improve Learning & Teaching (https://www.edx.org/course/ introduction-to-data-wise-a-collaborative-process)
Cost	Free (open)—verified certificate (paid)
Duration	2 weeks
Expected workload to study the course	4–6 hours a week
Learning objectives	Understand what the data wise improvement process is and how it can help you improve teaching and learning Build skills in looking at a wide range of data sources, including test scores, student work, and teaching practice Identify next steps in supporting a culture of collaborative data inquiry in your setting As a bonus, this course provides a complete video case study introducing the Universal Data Wise Improvement Process and showing how it can be used at a system level
Link with existing EDL competence framework	–
Structure	Step 1—Organize for collaborative work Step 2—Build assessment literacy Step 3—Create data overview Step 4—Dig into student data Step 5—Examine instruction Step 6—Develop action plan Step 7—Plan to assess Progress Step 8—Act and assess
Method of assessment	Self-assessment
Comment why this is a useful course to include in the review	Upon completion of this course, learners will be able to pursue opportunities for continuing to learn and apply the data wise improvement process

Title of the course	[10] Using Data to Provide Personalized Student Support (https://www. edx. org/ course/ using-data-provide-personalized-student- utarlingtonx-link-la-ssax)
Type of course	University course
Targeted audience	Educational designers, learning technology managers, and academics
Offered by	University of Texas Arlington via edX
Means of delivery	MOOC
Cost	Free (open)—verified certificate (paid)
Duration	3 weeks
Expected workload to study the course	5–7 hours per week

(continued)

Title of the course	[10] Using Data to Provide Personalized Student Support (https://www.edx.org/course/using-data-provide-personalized-student- utarlingtonx-link-la-ssax)
Learning objectives	How data sets are captured in learning experiences What basic procedures to use to manipulate these data sets The use of statistical models to predict student behavior The deployment of personalized support actions for the students
Link with existing EDL competence framework	–
Structure	Week 1: Computer logs Week 2: From logs to indicators Week 3: Combining data sources and deploying student support actions
Method of assessment	Not mentioned
Comment why this is a useful course to include in the review	This course will guide learners on how can data be translated into actionable knowledge and how can data help improve the overall quality of a learning experience.

Title of the course	[11] Trusted Learning Analytics (https://www.ou.nl/en/-/mooc-trusted-learning-analytics)
Type of course	University course
Targeted audience	Not mentioned
Offered by	Open Universiteit (*OUNL*, the Netherlands) via OpenEdX
Means of delivery	MOOC
Cost	Free
Duration	4 weeks
Expected workload to study the course	4–5 hours per week
Learning objectives	This course aims at framing learning analytics and its most important dimensions. It will demonstrate why learning analytics has the power to be a real game-changer for educational research by enhancing the e-learning experiences and creating more effective e-learning environments.
Link with existing EDL competence framework	–

(continued)

Title of the course	[11] Trusted Learning Analytics (https://www.ou.nl/en/-/mooc-trusted-learning-analytics)

Structure	*Welcome*
	  Course introduction
	  Make your own plan
	Week 1: Grounding: LA in a Nutshell
	  Intro + grounding video
	  Definition and dimensions of LA
	  References
	  Assignment: Getting started with LA
	Week 2: Digging: LA implementation challenges
	  Intro + digging video
	  Ethics and privacy
	  LA for learning design
	  Evaluating LA
	  References
	  Assignment: Quiz
	Week 3: Peeling: Learning analytics dashboards
	  Intro + peeling video
	  Dashboard design
	  Dashboard interpretation
	  LA case studies
	  References
	  Assignment: Evaluating a LA dashboard
	Week 4: Shining: Create your own LA
	  Intro + shining video
	  Final assignment: Design your own learning analytics

Method of assessment	Peer assessment + online quiz
Comment why this is a useful course to include in the review	This course has an interesting part of planning own study. Planning reminders are set according to this plan. The course has interesting peer assessing assignments. After submitting an assignment, participants are required to evaluate the answers submitted by two of their peers.

Title of the course	[12] Learning Analytics in Higher Education (https://www.edx.org/course/moving-towards-systematic-adoption-of-learning-analytics-in-higher-education)
Type of course	University course
Targeted audience	Not mentioned

(continued)

Title of the course	[12] Learning Analytics in Higher Education (https://www.edx.org/course/moving-towards-systematic-adoption-of-learning-analytics-in-higher-education)
Offered by	Universidad Carlos III de Madrid via EdX Dragan Gašević, Professor of Learning Analytics. Monash University Carlos Delgado Kloos, Full Professor. Universidad Carlos III de Madrid. Pedro J. Muñoz-Merino, Associate Professor. Universidad Carlos III de Madrid Maren Scheffel, Assistant Professor. Open University of the Netherlands Hendrik Drachsler, Professor. University of Frankfurt & German Leibniz Institute of Education (DIPF) Kairit Tammets, Senior Researcher. Tallinn University Yi-Shan Tsai, Research Associate. University of Edinburgh Anaïs Gourdin, Project Manager. European Association for Quality Assurance in Higher Education (ENQA) Rasmus Benke-Åberg, Director. Erasmus Student Network (ESN)
Means of delivery	MOOC
Cost	Free course auditing—verified certificate (paid)
Duration	3 weeks
Expected workload to study the course	3–5 hours per week
Learning objectives	What you'll learn Describe and critically discuss the current state of learning analytics in higher education Outline and analyze the adoption of learning analytics in an international landscape Explain and appraise key drivers, challenges, and relevant policies Apply the SHEILA framework for learning analytics strategy formation Apply the SHEILA framework for learning analytics policy formation Address and manage different expectations and concerns among stakeholders
Link with existing EDL competence framework	SHEILA framework

(continued)

Title of the course	[12] Learning Analytics in Higher Education (https://www.edx.org/course/moving-towards-systematic-adoption-of-learning-analytics-in-higher-education)
Structure	Week 1: Learning analytics in higher education: Overview (a) The rise of learning analytics in higher education (b) The global landscape of adoption (c) Success and challenges in the adoption of learning analytics in higher education (d) Ethics and privacy issues (e) Learning analytics policies (f) Using learning analytics for quality assurance Week 2: Enabling systematic adoption using SHEILA framework (b) SHEILA framework—Steps and tools (c) Key actions towards a systematic adoption (d) Key challenges to address (e) Key questions to answer when developing an institutional policy or strategy (f) Using SHEILA framework—Case studies Week 3: Adopting learning analytics in a complex educational system (a) Cultural differences in stakeholder expectations (b) Managing multi-stakeholder expectations (c) Working together with different stakeholders (d) A systematic adoption of learning analytics in higher education
Method of assessment	The evaluation is based on two tests in weeks 1 and 2 (they are graded with a 35% each) about the contents and one activity in week 3 (graded with a 30%). To pass the course it will be necessary to obtain the 60% of the final grade.
Comment why this is a useful course to include in the review	This course gives an overview of learning analytics in higher education and introduces the SHEILA framework that can be used to support strategy and policy formation in addition to readiness assessment.

Title of the course	[13] Learning Analytics Unraveled (https://www.maastrichtuniversity.nl/learning- analytics-unraveled)
Type of course	University course
Targeted audience	N/A

Offered by	Maastricht University, Next Learning Valley and The Learning Hub
	    Simon Beausaert, Associate Professor in Workplace Learning at Maastricht University
	    Melvyn Hamstra, Assistant Professor in Organizational Behavior at Maastricht University
	    Simeon De Simon, The Learning Hub
	    Francois Walgering, Next Learning Valley

Means of delivery	MOOC
Cost	Free
Duration	4 weeks
Expected workload to study the course	4 hours per week
Learning objectives	N/A

(continued)

Title of the course	[13] Learning Analytics Unraveled (https://www.maastrichtuniversity.nl/ learning- analytics-unraveled)
Link with existing EDL competence framework	–
Structure	*Week 1*: introduction on "what is learning analytics" and how could it be applied in different organizations *Week 2*: why we should be interested in learning analytics and for which kind of purposes it can be used *Week 3*: different ways of applying learning analytics *Week 4*: Pitfalls when doing learning analytics
Method of assessment	N/A
Comment why this is a useful course to include in the review	MOOC on Learning Analytics Unraveled aims to help learners to understand what Learning Analytics is all about, why they should use it and how. After the completion of the course learners will know about all the LA ins and outs and have a better understanding of implementing it in an organization.

Title of the course	[14] Analytics in Course Design: Leveraging Canvas Data (He) (https:// www.canvas.net/browse/dartmouth/courses/analytics-in-course-design)
Type of course	Professional development
Targeted audience	Faculty and instructional designers of Dartmouth College
Offered by	Dartmouth College via canvas **Jing Qi, EdD**, LMS and Learning Analytic Specialist at Dartmouth College, NH. **Brian Reid, PhD**, Associate Director of Information Technology at Geisel School of Medicine at Dartmouth
Means of delivery	Online course
Cost	Free
Duration	6 hours
Expected workload to study the course	6 hours in total

(continued)

Title of the course	[14] Analytics in Course Design: Leveraging Canvas Data (He) (https://www.canvas.net/browse/dartmouth/courses/analytics-in-course-design)
Learning objectives	Upon completing this course, participants should be able to: Install a userscript that gathers the access report data for an entire course Understand the common fields included in the Access Report raw data Load the data to an app that analyzes the access report data Understand content usage in a course, and apply the results to improve course design that better facilitates student engagements Understand canvas course design strategy categories Install an userscript that evaluates the design strategies being applied in a course Deploy a mixed course design strategy to facilitate greater engagement and better learning Install an userscript that gathers quiz submission data in a course Understand the common fields that are included in the quiz submission raw data Analyze the quiz submission data to address the questions which are not answered in the Canvas built-in quiz statistics Install an userscript that gathers discussion data for an entire course Understand the common fields included in the discussion raw data Create an edge list that includes from (reply_author) and to (initial_thread_author) fields, and load the discussion data to a discussion analytical app Use the diagrams to inform student discussion participation and facilitate greater discussion engagement
Link with existing EDL competence framework	–
Structure	This course contains four modules that each applies different aspects of canvas data to canvas course design. They include: 1. *Course engagements*: Leverage the student Access Report to analyze course content engagements 2. *Course content design*: Explore the usage of Canvas course features and the organization of course navigation items to categorize canvas course design strategies 3. *Assignment submissions*: Examine assignment and quiz submission data using an analytical approach 4. *Discussion interactions*: Analyze student participation using canvas discussion data to help faculty understand how students interacted with their peers in canvas discussion forums and whether they were actively engaged in discussions
Method of assessment	N/A
Comment why this is a useful course to include in the review	This course is useful for leveraging Canvas Data and visualization techniques to make informed decisions about Canvas course design.

(continued)

Title of the course	[15] NOC: Introduction To Learning Analytics (https://nptel.ac.in/courses/127/101/127101012/)
Type of course	University course
Targeted audience	University students
Offered by	IIT Bombay via NPTEL
Means of delivery	Online course (video lectures only)
Cost	Free course auditing
Duration	4 weeks
Expected workload to study the course	40 min per week
Learning objectives	N/A
Link with existing EDL competence framework	–

Structure	Week 1: What is LA
	   Definition
	   Relation with academic analytics
	   Relation with education data mining
	   LA—Big-picture
	   Relation with machine learning, EDM
	   Four levels of learning analytics
	   Overview I
	   Overview—II
	Week 2: Data collection
	   How big is education data
	   Data collection from learning environments
	   Preprocessing ethics in learning analytics
	   Student privacy
	Week 3: Descriptive analytics
	   Data visualization example dashboard analytics
	Week 4: Predictive analytics
	   Linear regression analytics tools
	   Demo of Weka/Rapidminer
	   Demo of linear regression using Weka

Method of assessment	Exams
Comment why this is a useful course to include in the review	This course is useful as a LA course example from a non-western country.

Title of the course	[16] Learning Analytics and Knowledge LAK13 (https://learn.canvas.net/courses/33)
Type of course	Professional development
Targeted audience	This course will be of interest to individuals across the full learning spectrum: K- 12, higher education, corporate learning and informal/lifelong learning. Leaders, educators, and even students will benefit from the topics explored and the related implementation issues (in particular, privacy and ethics of analytics)

(continued)

Title of the course	[16] Learning Analytics and Knowledge LAK13 (https://learn.canvas.net/courses/33)
Offered by	Canvas taught by: Simon Buckingham Shum (Open University UK) Shane Dawson (University of South Australia) Erik Duval (Katholieke Universiteit Leuven) Dragan Gašević (Athabasca University) George Siemens (Athabasca University)
Means of delivery	MOOC
Cost	Free
Duration	8 weeks
Expected workload to study the course	5–10 hours per week
Learning objectives	After completing this course, participants will be able to: 1. Describe learning analytics and how it differs from related concepts such as educational datamining and academic analytics 2. Analyze, plan, and deploy a small learning analytics pilot, including the intent of LA and tools needed to address analytics goals 3. Develop a matrix of prominent learning analytics tools and the particular analytics strategies each tool addresses 4. Evaluate current state of learning analytics technologies and describe the benefits and drawbacks to open source and proprietary tool sets 5. Evaluate and describe the role of semantic web and linked data in next generation educational content 6. Conduct basic analytics activities (such as importing and visualizing data) through in open source tools (R) and commercial tools (Tableau Software)
Link with existing EDL competence framework	–
Structure	*Week 1*: Trends and context: Why learning analytics? *Week 2*: Cases and examples of implementation of learning analytics *Week 3*: Tools, methods, and levels of learning analytics *Week 4*: Predictive models & assessment *Week 5*: Smarter curriculum: semantic web, linked data, and adaptive content *Week 6*: Epistemology, pedagogy, assessment and learning analytics *Week 7*: Privacy and ethics: Principles for governing LA use and implementation *Week 8*: Learning analytics: where is it headed? How to get involved (SoLAR, IEDMS, academic programs)
Method of assessment	Not mentioned
Comment why this is a useful course to include in the review	This course will provide a (generally non-technical) introduction to learning analytics and how they are being deployed in various contexts in the education field. Additionally, the tools and methods, ethics and privacy, and the systemic impact of analytics will be explored, presenting a broad overview of the current state and possible future directions of the field.

(continued)

Title of the course	[17] Using Data to Improve Student Outcomes (https://www.futurelearn.com/courses/data-student-outcomes)
Type of course	Professional development
Targeted audience	This course is designed for professional educators, as well as those working in other professional services like health, who wish to use data science to improve outcomes
Offered by	American Association of Colleges for teacher Education (AACTE) via FutureLearn
Means of delivery	MOOC
Cost	Free course auditing verified certificate (paid)
Duration	3 weeks
Expected workload to study the course	3 hours per week
Learning objectives	By the end of the course, you'll be able to: Identify data sources and recognize different types of data Recognize and discuss different methods for improvement initiatives Interpret case studies and discuss improvement processes within your own context and professional experience Explain the relationship between data, findings and actions required in or to achieve continuous improvement Describe the difference between data and findings Produce findings from a sample set of data Evaluate and discuss the different approaches taken in example data dashboards Identify and select the most appropriate indicators for measuring improvement
Link with existing EDL competence framework	–
Structure	Week 1—Improvement science Identifying different sources and types of data Ways to improve student outcomes Improvement processes in your own context and professional experience Real-world examples of improving student outcomes Week 2—Findings How to present and evaluate data effectively The difference between data and findings The role of ethics in data handling and sharing The relationship required between data, findings and actions, to achieve continuous improvement Week 3—Actions Different indicators for measuring improvement How to collect sample data and select the appropriate indicator How to present indicators and actions to students
Method of assessment	Not mentioned

(continued)

Title of the course	[17] Using Data to Improve Student Outcomes (https://www.futurelearn.com/courses/data-student-outcomes)
Comment why this is a useful course to include in the review	This free online course from AACTE American Association of Colleges for Teacher Education (a national alliance of educator preparation dedicated to offering high-quality, evidence-based programs) claims that it will help learners to use data science to deliver better outcomes for their students.

Title of the course	[18] Learning analytics: process and theory (http://www.drps.ed.ac.uk/20-21/dpt/cxedua11339.htm)
Type of course	University course
Targeted audience	University students
Offered by	The University of Edinburgh Course leader: Professor Dragan Gasevic
Means of delivery	Online course
Cost	Fees are applied
Duration	Not mentioned
Expected workload to study the course	Not mentioned
Learning objectives	On completion of the course you will be able to: Describe and critically analyse learning analytics process and theory; Review, integrate and critically assess emerging trends in learning analytics literature; Develop a proposal for a piece of research or application using learning analytics in an educational setting, based in a critical understanding of the literature Develop a detailed plan for the learning analytics application or research proposed, and critically assess its main elements
Link with existing EDL competence framework	–

(continued)

Title of the course	[18] Learning analytics: process and theory (http://www.drps.ed.ac.uk/20-21/dpt/cxedua11339.htm)
Structure	The course is structured around a number of activities. Each week will have a set of readings introducing the topics of learning analytics covered by the course. The topics will be adjusted each to acknowledge the rapid development of the field of learning analytics and its theory and processes. Each of these readings will be accompanied by a series of tutor-provided questions that will help scaffold participants' posts to asynchronous online discussion posts. The purpose of these discussions is to create a space for the participants to engage with social knowledge construction activities, negotiate the meaning of the topics studied with their peers, and get to appreciate and critical discuss different viewpoints to learning analytics. Each summative assessment will be accompanied with formative feedback to inform and guide later assessments in the course. The three main assessments guide the participants through a process of the development of their ideas—from early literature review to project proposal to project execution, and reporting and presentation of the findings. To increase the flexibility necessary to a globally-distributed cohort, online activities are mainly asynchronous. To increase access to the tutor, the course will feature weekly synchronous discussion session with the instructor and scheduled weekly online chats.
Method of assessment	Assignments are designed to be cumulative while remaining distinct *Assignment 1*: Critical literature review paper (35% of your final mark) *Assignment 2*: Collaborative formulation of application or research proposal (20% of your final mark) *Assignment 3*: Learning analytics planning paper (40% of your final mark)
Comment why this is a useful course to include in the review	This course provides a framework for understanding and critically discussing the emerging field of learning analytics. Students will learn about the distinction between learning analytics, educational data mining, and big data, and the relationship of learning analytics and existing fields perspectives on what learning analytics should be will be connected to philosophy and theory on the nature of design and inquiry. Learners will consider what it means for a learning analytics analysis or model to be valid, and the key challenges to the effective and appropriate use of learning analytics.

Appendix B.2—Learning Objectives and Syllabus per Course Mapped to the Identified Dimensions

Learning Objectives as reported in syllabus	Courses
Define reliability and validity in classroom terms [D.1c] Define data literacy and explain why educators need to be data literate [D7] Give good reasons why educators don't necessarily jump up and down with excitement about data and assessment [D2] Know what you can do to own and spread the data literacy story in your context [D7] Recognize that data are more than standardized test scores [D1.a] Gather [D1.b] four types of data in your own context Reinforce and support your learning and data literacy development [D7] Define classroom research and how it might improve learning in your classroom and/or school [D5.a] Generate and share potential research questions [D5.a] Identify appropriate data sources for conducting your research [D1.b]	[1] Data Literacy 01
How educational data analytics can improve classroom teaching and learning, as well as supporting data-driven decision making at various levels of school operations [D5.b] An understanding of the current state-of-the-art in teaching and learning analytics tools and methods [D8] How teaching analytics can be used to analyse your lesson plans [D3.a] How learning analytics can be used to analyse the classroom delivery of your lesson plan and reveal more about your students' learning [D3.a] How you can reflect on your teaching practice by combining Insights from both teaching and learning analytics [D5.a]	[2] Analytics for the Classroom Teacher
The field of learning analytics and explore how data and information are used [D8] Common learning analytics methods and approaches, such as data wrangling and cleaning [D2.a], structure discovery, and basic prediction modelling [D3.a] How to conduct basic data wrangling [D2.a] and analyses [D3.a] Ethics and privacy considerations [D6.b] Working in a collaborative, cross-disciplinary setting Common toolsets used in the UTArlingtonX Learning Analytics courses (R in RStudio and Jupiter Notebooks) [D10.a]	[3] Learning Analytics Fundamentals
Key methods for educational data mining [D3.a] How to apply methods using standard tools such as RapidMiner [D10.c] How to use methods to answer practical educational questions [D5.b]	[4] Big Data and Education

(continued)

Learning Objectives as reported in syllabus	Courses
How to identify trade-offs between proprietary and opensource tools commonly used in learning analytics **[D10]** The learning analytics data cycle **[D8]** How to perform social network analysis, interpret the analysis for the study of networked learning, and visualize the analysis results in **Gephi [D10.d]** Training and evaluating classifiers that use clickstream data, with a focus on how to engineer features and training labels Evaluation issues, key diagnostic metrics and their uses, and validity issues **[D5.a]** How to approach a problem in the area of text mining using *LightSIDE*, how to engineer features for text classification, how to use *LightSIDE* for automated collaborative learning process analysis **[D10.e]** How trained models can be used in service of learning research **[D5.b]**	[5] Data, Analytics and Learning (not available anymore)
About the landscape of learning analytics in higher education **[D8]** How to bring in data of your own for analysis and visualization **[D3.a, D3.b]** About performance prediction in a course: up to and including grade penalties, placement analyses, performance disparities and their correlates, course-to-course correlation **[D5.a]** How institutions are creating early warning systems and personalized communication **[D5.c]** How to apply learning analytics to observe differences and Probe impact, capturing more and better information **[D5.a]**	[6] Practical Learning Analytics
To understand and use data effectively **[D7]** To inform teaching and learning decisions **[D5.b]**	[7] Data Literacy for School Teachers—EDPZ6012
Train participants in data literacy skills **[D7]** Efficient collection of data and metadata for future analyses **[D1]** Data wrangling, tidying, and organization in **R [D2.a, D10.a]** Data visualization and analysis in **R [D3.a, D3.b D10.a]** Teach participants basic tools for reproducible science reproducible report creation version control **[D10]** Introduce participants to Open Science principles and procedures Data archiving options and best practice **[D2.c]** Code sharing options and best practice Introduce participants to the fundamentals of programming basics in R **[D10.a]** The principles of tidy code and code review Create a community of data literate scientists **[D7]**	[8] Advancing computational and data literacy skills schools for life scientists (not available anymore)
Understand what the Data Wise Improvement Process is and how it can help you improve teaching and learning **[D7]** Build skills in looking at a wide range of data sources, including test scores, student work, and teaching practice **[D1.a, D1.b]** Identify next steps in supporting a culture of collaborative Data inquiry in your setting **[D5.b]** As a bonus, this course provides a complete video case study introducing the universal data wise improvement process and showing how it can be used at a system level	[9] Introduction to Data Wise: A Collaborative Process to Improve Learning & Teaching

(continued)

Learning Objectives as reported in syllabus	Courses
How data sets are captured in learning experiences **[D1]** What basic procedures to use to manipulate these data sets **[D2]** The use of statistical models to predict student behavior **[D4.b]** The deployment of personalized support actions for the students **[D5.c]**	[10] Using Data to Provide Personalized Student Support

This course aims at framing learning analytics and its most important dimensions. It will demonstrate why learning analytics has the power to be a real game-changer for educational research by enhancing the e-learning experiences and creating more effective e-learning environments **[D8]**
Welcome
  Course introduction
  Make your own plan
Week 1: Grounding: LA in a Nutshell
  Intro + grounding video
  Definition and dimensions of LA
  References
  Assignment: Getting started with LA
Week 2: Digging: LA implementation challenges
  Intro + digging video
  Ethics and privacy **[D6.b]**
  LA for learning design
  Evaluating LA
  References
  Assignment: Quiz
Week 3: Peeling: Learning analytics dashboards
  Intro + peeling video
  Dashboard design **[D3.b]**
  Dashboard interpretation **[D4]**
  LA case studies
  References
  Assignment: Evaluating a LA dashboard
Week 4: Shining: Create your own LA
  Intro + shining video
Final assignment: Design your own learning analytics
	[11] Trusted Learning Analytics

(continued)

Learning Objectives as reported in syllabus	Courses

Describe and critically discuss the current state of learning analytics in higher education **[D8]**
Outline and analyze the adoption of learning analytics in an international landscape **[D8]**
Explain and appraise key drivers, challenges, and relevant policies
Apply the *SHEILA* framework for learning analytics strategy formation **[D9.a]**
Apply the *SHEILA* framework for learning analytics policy formation **[D9.a]**
Address and manage different expectations and concerns among stakeholders
Week 1: Learning Analytics in Higher Education: Overview
  (a) The rise of learning analytics in higher education
  (b) The global landscape of adoption
  (c) Success and challenges in the adoption of learning analytics in higher education
  (d) Ethics and privacy issues **[D6.b]**
  (e) Learning analytics policies
  (f) Using learning analytics for quality assurance.
Week 2: Enabling systematic adoption using SHEILA framework
  (a) SHEILA framework—Steps and tools **[D9.a]**
  (b) Key actions towards a systematic adoption
  (c) Key challenges to address
  (d) Key questions to answer when developing an institutional policy or strategy
  (e) Using SHEILA framework—Case studies
Week 3: Adopting learning analytics in a complex educational system
  (a) Cultural differences in stakeholder expectations
  (b) Managing multi-stakeholder expectations
  (c) Working together with different stakeholders
  (d) A systematic adoption of learning analytics in higher education
	[12] Learning Analytics in Higher Education

MOOC on Learning Analytics Unraveled aims to help us to understand what Learning Analytics is all about, why we should use it and how. After the completion of the course we will know about all the LA ins and outs and have a better understanding of implementing it in an organization **[D8]** *Week 1*: Introduction on 'what is learning analytics' and how could it be applied in different organizations *Week 2*: Why we should be interested in learning analytics and for which kind of purposes it can be used *Week 3*: Different ways of applying learning analytics *Week 4*: Pitfalls when doing learning analytics	[13] Learning Analytics Unraveled

(continued)

Learning Objectives as reported in syllabus	Courses
Install an userscript that gathers the *Access Report* data for an entire course **[D1.a, D1.b]** Understand the common fields included in the the *Access Report* raw data **[D2]** Load the data to an app that analyzes the *Access Report* data **[D3]** Understand content usage in a course **[D4]**, and apply the results to improve course design that better facilitates student engagements **[D5]** Understand **canvas** course design strategy categories **[D11.b]** Install an userscript that evaluates the design strategies being applied in a course **[D5.a]** Deploy a mixed course design strategy to facilitate greater engagement and better learning **[D5.a]** Install an userscript that gathers quiz submission data in a course **[D1.b]** Understand the common fields that are included in the *quiz submission* raw data **[D2]** Analyze the *quiz submission* data to address the questions which are not answered in the canvas built-in quiz statistics **[D3.a]** Install an userscript that gathers discussion data for an entire course **[D1.b]** Understand the common fields included in the *discussion* raw data **[D2]** Create an edge list that includes from (reply_author) and to (initial_thread_author) fields, and load the **discussion** data to a discussion analytical app **[D3.a]** Use the diagrams **[D3.b]** to inform student discussion participation **[D4.c]** and facilitate greater discussion Engagement **[D5.a]**	[14] Analytics in Course Design: Leveraging Canvas Data (HE)

(continued)

Learning Objectives as reported in syllabus	Courses

COURSE PLAN:
Week 1: **[D8]**
  What is LA
  Definition
  Relation with academic analytics
  Relation with education data mining
  Learning LA—Big-picture
  Relation with machine learning, EDM
  Four levels of learning analytics
  Overview I
  Overview—II
Week 2: **[D1]**, **[D2]**, **[D6]**
  Data collection
  How big is education data
  Data collection from learning environments
  Preprocessing
  Ethics in learning analytics
  Student privacy
Week 3: **[D3]**
  Descriptive analytics
  Data visualization example
  Dashboard analytics
Week 4: **[D5]**, **[D10]**
  Predictive analytics
  Linear regression
  Analytics tools
  Demo of Weka/Rapidminer
  Demo of linear regression using Weka
	[15] NOC: Introduction to Learning Analytics

(continued)

Learning Objectives as reported in syllabus	Courses
At the conclusion of this course, participants will be able to: 1. Describe learning analytics and how it differs from related concepts such as educational data mining and academic analytics **[D8]** 2. Analyze, plan, and deploy a small learning analytics pilot, including the intent of LA and tools needed to address analytics goals **[D5]** 3. Develop a matrix of prominent learning analytics tools and the particular analytics strategies each tool addresses 4. Evaluate current state of learning analytics technologies and describe the benefits and drawbacks to open source and proprietary tool sets 5. Evaluate and describe the role of semantic web and linked data in next generation educational content 6. Conduct basic analytics activities (such as importing and visualizing data) through in open source tools (R) and commercial tools (tableau software) **[D1.a, D1.b, D1.c, D3.b, D10.a]** *Week 1*: Trends and context: Why learning analytics? *Week 2*: Cases and examples of implementation of learning analytics **[D8]** *Week 3*: Tools, methods, and levels of learning analytics *Week 4*: Predictive models & assessment *Week 5*: Smarter curriculum: Semantic web, linked data, and adaptive content *Week 6*: Epistemology, pedagogy, assessment, and learning analytics *Week 7*: Privacy and ethics: Principles for governing LA use and implementation **[D6.b]** *Week 8*: Learning analytics: where is it headed? How to get involved (SoLAR, IEDMS, academic programs)	[16] Learning Analytics and Knowledge LAK13

(continued)

Learning Objectives as reported in syllabus	Courses

Identify data sources and recognize different types of data [D1]
Recognize and discuss different methods for improvement initiatives [D5]
Interpret case studies and discuss improvement processes within your own context and professional experience [D4]
Explain the relationship between data, findings and actions required in order to achieve continuous improvement [D5]
Describe the difference between data and findings
Produce findings from a sample set of data [D3]
Evaluate and discuss the different approaches taken in example data dashboards [D4]
Identify and select the most appropriate indicators for measuring improvement [D5]
Week 1—Improvement science
    Identifying different sources and types of data [D1]
    Ways to improve student outcomes
    Improvement processes in your own context and professional experience
    Real-world examples of improving student outcomes
Week 2—Findings
    How to present and evaluate data effectively [D3]
    The difference between data and findings [D3]
    The role of ethics in data handling and sharing [D6]
    The relationship required between data, findings and actions, to achieve continuous improvement
Week 3—Actions
    Different indicators for measuring improvement [D5]
    How to collect sample data and select the appropriate indicator [D1]
    How to present indicators and actions to students
	[17] Using Data to Improve Student Outcomes (not available anymore)

Describe and critically analyse learning analytics process and theory; [D8] Review, integrate and critically assess emerging trends in learning analytics literature; [D8] Develop a proposal for a piece of research or application using learning analytics in an educational setting, based in a critical understanding of the literature [D8] Develop a detailed plan for the learning analytics application or research proposed, and critically assess its main elements [D5]	[18] Learning Analytics: Process and Theory

(continued)

References

Anderson, L., Krathwohl, D., & Bloom, B. (2001). *A taxonomy for learning, teaching, and assessing: A revision of Bloom's taxonomy of educational objectives*. Longman.

Berson, A., & Dubov, L. (2010). *Master data management and data governance* (2nd ed.). McGraw-Hill Education.

Cady, F. (2017). *The data science handbook* (1st ed.). Wiley.

Clark, K., Duckham, M., Guillemin, M., Hunter, A., McVernon, J., O'Keefe, C., Pitkin, C., Prawer, S., Sinnott, R., Warr, D., & Waycott, J. (2015). *Guidelines for the ethical use of digital data in human research*. The University of Melbourne.

Data Quality Campaign. (2014). *Teacher data literacy: It's about time: A brief for state policy makers*. Washington, DC: Author.

Demchenko, I., & Belloum, A. (2017, July). *EDISON: Discussion document: Part 1. Data Science Competence Framework (CF-DS) release 2* (pp. 1–59). https://doi.org/10.5281/ZENODO.1044346

European Commission. (2016, June 10). Communication from the Commission to the European Parliament, the Council, The European Economic and Social Committee and the Committee of the Regions on A New Skills Agenda for Europe: Working together to strengthen human capital, employability and competitiveness. COM(2016) 381 final. Brussels. Retrieved from: https://eur-lex.europa.eu/legal-content/EN/TXT/?uri=CELEX:52016DC0381

European Commission. (2018, January 17). Communication from the Commission to the European Parliament, the Council, The European Economic and Social Committee and the Committee of the Regions on the Digital Education Action Plan. COM(2018) 22 final. Brussels. Retrieved from: https://eur-lex.europa.eu/legal-content/EN/TXT/?uri=COM:2018:22:FIN

European Commission. (2020a, August 30). Communication from the Commission to the European Parliament, the Council, The European Economic and Social Committee and the Committee of the Regions on the Digital Education Action Plan 2021–2027: Resetting education and training for the digital age. COM(2020) 624 final. Brussels. Retrieved from: https://eur-lex.europa.eu/legal-content/EN/TXT/?uri=CELEX%3A52020DC0624

European Commission. (2020b). Commission Staff Working Document. Communication from the Commission to the European Parliament, the Council, the European Economic and Social Committee and the Committee of the Regions: Digital Education Action Plan 2021–2027 Resetting education and training for the digital age. Retrieved from: https://ec.europa.eu/education/sites/education/files/document-library-docs/deap-swd-sept2020_en.pdf%23page25

D. Sampson et al., *Educational Data Literacy*, Advances in Analytics for Learning and Teaching, https://doi.org/10.1007/978-3-031-11705-3

European Commission. (2020c). Communication from the Commission to the European Parliament, the Council, the European Economic and Social Committee and the Committee of the Regions on achieving the European Education Area by 2025 Retrieved from: https://ec.europa.eu/education/sites/default/files/document-library-docs/communication-european-education-area.pdf

Hamilton, L., Halverson, R., Jackson, S., Mandinach, E., Supovitz, J., & Wayman, J. (2009). *Using student achievement data to support instructional decision making (NCEE 2009-4067).* National Center for Education Evaluation and Regional Assistance, Institute of Education Sciences, U.S. Department of Education. Retrieved from: https://ies.ed.gov/ncee/wwc/Docs/PracticeGuide/dddm_pg_092909.pdf

Hon Matt Hancock. (2018). *Data ethics framework, UK Ministerial Foreword.*

Ikemoto, G. S., & Marsh, J. A. (2007). Cutting through the data decision mantra: Different conception of data-driven decision making. In P. A. Moss (Ed.), *Evidence and decision making* (pp. 105–131). Blackwell.

Kampylis, P., Punie, Y., & Devine, J. (2015). *Promoting effective digital-age learning – A European framework for digitally-competent educational Organisations; EUR 27599 EN.* European Joint Research Centre (JRC).

Knapp, M. S., Swinnerton, J. A., Copland, M. A., & Monpas-Huber, J. (2006). *Data-informed leadership in education.* University of Washington, Center for the Study of Teaching and Policy.

Lai, M., & Schildkamp, K. (2013). Data-based decision making: An overview. In K. Schildkamp, M. Lai, & L. Earl (Eds.), *Data-based decision making in education* (Studies in educational leadership) (Vol. 17). Springer.

Love, N. (2012). *Data literacy for teachers.* Hawker Brownlow Education.

Mandinach, E. B. (2012). A perfect time for data use: Using data-driven decision making to inform practice. *Educational Psychologist, 47*(2), 71–85. https://doi.org/10.1080/00461520.2012.667064

Mandinach, E. B., & Gummer, E. S. (2013). A systemic view of implementing data literacy in educator preparation. *Educational Researcher, 42*(1), 30–37. https://doi.org/10.3102/0013189X12459803

Mandinach, E. B., & Gummer, E. S. (2016). What does it mean for teachers to be data literate: Laying out the skills, knowledge, and dispositions. *Teaching and Teacher Education, 60,* 366–376. https://doi.org/10.1016/j.tate.2016.07.011

Mandinach, E. B., Friedman, J. M., & Gummer, E. S. (2015). How can schools of education help to build educators' capacity to use data? A systemic view of the issue. *Teachers College Record, 117*(4), 1–50. https://doi.org/10.1177/016146811511700404

Marsh, J. A. (2012). Interventions promoting educators' use of data: Research insights and gaps. *Teachers College Record, 114*(11), 1–48.

Marsh, J. A., & Farrell, C. C. (2015). How leaders can support teachers with data-driven decision making: A framework for understanding capacity building. *Educational Management Administration & Leadership, 43*(2), 269–289. https://doi.org/10.1177/1741143214537229

Means, B., Chen, E., DeBarger, A., & Padilla, C. (2011). *Teachers' ability to use data to inform instruction: Challenges and supports.* Office of Planning, Evaluation and Policy Development, U.S. Department of Education.

Mortier, R., Haddadi, H., Henderson, T., McAuley, D., & Crowcroft, J. (2014). *Human–data interaction: The human face of the data-driven society.* SSRN Electronic Journal 10.2139/ssrn.2508051.

North Carolina Department of Public Instruction. (2013). *Data literacy.* Retrieved from http://ites.ncdpi.wikispaces.net/Data+Literacy

OECD. (2016). *Innovating education and educating for innovation: The power of digital technologies and skills.* OECD Publishing. https://doi.org/10.1787/9789264265097-en

Papamitsiou, Z., Filippakis, M., Poulou, M., Sampson, D. G., Ifenthaler, D., & Giannakos, M. (2021). Towards an educational data literacy framework: Enhancing the profiles of instructional designers and e-tutors of online and blended courses with new competences. *Smart Learning Environments, 8,* 18. https://doi.org/10.1186/s40561-021-00163-w

Prado, C. J., & Marzal, A. M. (2013). Incorporating data literacy into information literacy programs: Core competencies and contents. *Libri, 63*(2), 123–134. https://doi.org/10.1515/libri-2013-0010

Redecker, C. (2017). European framework for the digital competence of educators: DigCompEdu. In Y. Punie (Ed.), *EUR 28775 EN*. Publications Office of the European Union. https://doi.org/10.2760/159770. ISBN 978-92-79-73494-6, JRC107466.

Reimers, F. M., Schleicher, A., & Ansah, G. A. (2020). *Schooling disrupted, schooling rethought: How the Covid-19 pandemic is changing education.* OECD. Retrieved from: https://read.oecd-ilibrary.org/view/?ref=133_133390-1rtuknc0hi&title=Schooling-disrupted-schooling-rethought-How-the-Covid-19-pandemic-is-changing-education

Ridsdale, C., Rothwell, J., Smit, M., Ali-Hassan, H., Bliemel, M., Irvine, D., et al. (2015). *Strategies and best practices for data literacy education.* Dalhousie University.

Sampson, D., & Fytros, D. (2008). Competence models in technology-enhanced competence-based learning. In H. H. Adelsberger, Kinshuk, J. M. Pawlowski, & D. G. Sampson (Eds.), *International handbook on information technologies for education and training* (2nd ed., pp. 155–177). Springer.

Schildkamp, K., & Kuiper, W. (2010). Data-informed curriculum reform: Which data, what purposes, and promoting and hindering factors. *Teaching and Teacher Education, 26*(3), 482–496. https://doi.org/10.1016/j.tate.2009.06.007

Tattar, P., Ojeda, T., Murphy, S. P., Bengfort, B., & Dasgupta, A. (2017). *Practical data science cookbook – Second Edition: Data pre-processing, analysis and visualization using R and Python 2nd Revised edition Edition.* Packt Publishing.

The Information Accountability Foundation (IAF). (2015). *A unified ethical frame for big data analysis – Big data ethics initiative.* Retrieved from: https://secureservercdn.net/192.169.221.188/b1f.827.myftpupload.com/wp-content/uploads/2020/04/IAF-Big-Data-Ethics-Initiative-Part-B.pdf

The Open Data Institute (ODI). (2017). *The data ethics canvas.* Open Data Institute, London.

Tsai, Y.-S., Gašević, D., Whitelock-Wainwright, A., Muñoz-Merino, P. J., Moreno-Marcos, P. M., Fernández, A. R., Kloos, C. D., Scheffel, M., Jivet, I., Drachsler, H., Tammets, K., Calleja, A. R., & Kollom, K. (2018). *SHEILA: Supporting higher education to intergrade learning analytics research report.* Retrieved from: https://sheilaproject.eu/wp-content/uploads/2018/11/SHEILA-research-report.pdf

UNESCO. (2018). *UNESCO ICT competency framework for teachers.* UNESDOC Digital Library. Retrieved from https://unesdoc.unesco.org/ark:/48223/pf0000265721

United Nations Industrial Development Organization. (2015). *Human Resource Management Framework (HRMF).* s.l.:UNIDO/AI/2015/01. Retrieved from: https://www.unido.org/sites/default/files/2015-09/UNIDO-AI-2015-01_HRMF_0.pdf

Vahey, P., Yarnall, L., Patton, C., Zalles, D., & Swan, K. (2006). *Mathematizing middle school: Results from a cross-disciplinary study of data literacy.* In Annual Meeting of the American Educational Research Association, San Francisco, CA.

Vahey, P., Rafanan, K., Patton, C., Swan, K., van't Hooft, M., Kratcoski, A., & Stanford, T. (2012). A cross-disciplinary approach to teaching data literacy and proportionality. *Educational Studies in Mathematics, 81*, 179–205. https://doi.org/10.1007/s10649-012-9392-z

Wolff, A., Gooch, D., Cavero Montaner, J. J., Rashid, U., & Kortuem, G. (2016). Creating an understanding of data literacy for a data-driven society. *The Journal of Community Informatics, 12*(3), 9–26. Retrieved from: https://openjournals.uwaterloo.ca/index.php/JoCI/article/view/3275/4298

Zook, M., Barocas, S., Boyd, D., Crawford, K., Keller, E., Gangadharan, S. P., et al. (2017). Ten simple rules for responsible big data research. *PLoS Computational Biology, 13*(3), e1005399. https://doi.org/10.1371/journal.pcbi.1005399

Index

GPSR Compliance
The European Union's (EU) General Product Safety Regulation (GPSR) is a set
of rules that requires consumer products to be safe and our obligations to
ensure this.

If you have any concerns about our products, you can contact us on

ProductSafety@springernature.com

In case Publisher is established outside the EU, the EU authorized
representative is:

Springer Nature Customer Service Center GmbH
Europaplatz 3
69115 Heidelberg, Germany

www.ingramcontent.com/pod-product-compliance
Lightning Source LLC
Chambersburg PA
CBHW071014230525
27097CB00012B/150